66074

PN
6110
.C4
H5

Hill, Helen, 1915-.

New coasts & strange
harbors:
discovering poems

DATE			

New Coasts & Strange Harbors

Discovering Poems

New Coasts & Strange Harbors
Discovering Poems

Selected by Helen Hill and Agnes Perkins

Illustrated by Clare Romano and John Ross

Thomas Y. Crowell Company
New York

Manufactured in the United States of America
Copyright acknowledgments start on page v.

ISBN 0–690–00271–8

Library of Congress Cataloging in Publication Data
Hill, Helen, comp. New coasts & strange harbors.
    SUMMARY: An anthology of modern poems including
works by Philip Booth, Lucille Clifton, Galway Kinnell,
Robert Francis, Lillian Morrison, Richard Wilbur, e.e.
cummings, and many others.
    1. Children's poetry. [1. Poetry—Collections]
I. Perkins, Agnes, joint comp. II. Romano, Clare,
illus. III. Ross, John, 1921-   illus. IV. Title.
PN6110.C4H5   821'.008   74-12343
ISBN 0-690-00271-8

2 3 4 5 6 7 8 9 10

ACKNOWLEDGMENTS

We would like to express our thanks to a number of people who have been helpful to us as we have gathered these poems together: first, to our students with whom we have read many of the poems; second, to Professor Milton Foster for encouragement and support; and finally to Walter Clark, to Rebecca Hill Finney, and to our husbands, Donald Hill and David Perkins, for reading the manuscript and for suggesting some poems we are happy not to have missed.

In addition, acknowledgment is made to the following for permission to publish these poems:

October House, Inc., and Faber and Faber, Ltd., for "To My Mother," from *Collected Poems 1930 to 1965* by George Barker, copyright © 1957, 1962, and 1965 by George Granville Barker. Farrar, Straus & Giroux, Inc., for "Manners (for a Child of 1918)," "Little Exercise," "First Death in Nova Scotia," and "House Guest," from *The Complete Poems* by Elizabeth Bishop, copyright 1946, © 1955, 1962, 1968 by Elizabeth Bishop, copyright renewed 1974 by Elizabeth Bishop. Robert Bly, for "Driving Toward the Lac Qui Parle River," "A Late Spring Day in My Life," and "Watering the Horse," from *Silence in the Snowy Fields* by Robert Bly, copyright © 1962 by Robert Bly, published by Wesleyan University Press. The Viking Press, Inc., for "If It Comes" and "The Round," copyright © 1961 by Philip Booth, and "Was A Man," copyright © 1958 by Philip Booth, all from *The Islanders* by Philip Booth. Wesleyan University Press, for "Robin Hood," from *A Choice of Attitudes* by Gray Burr, copyright © 1969 by Gray Burr.

John Ciardi, for "Letter from A Death Bed" and "Romping," from *I Marry You* by John Ciardi, copyright © 1958 by Rutgers, The State University. Walter H. Clark, Jr., for his poem "Free Will," copyright © 1974 by Walter H. Clark, Jr., and for his poem "After Snow," first published in this volume. Commonweal Publishing Co., Inc., for "The Morning After" and "Uncle Death" by Walter H. Clark, Jr. Random House, Inc., for "Good Times," from *Good Times* by Lucille Clifton, copyright © 1969 by Lucille Clifton. Harcourt Brace Jovanovich, Inc., for the following from *Complete Poems 1913—1962* by E. E. Cummings: "buy me an ounce and i'll sell you a pound," copyright 1940 by E. E. Cummings, copyright © 1968 by Marion Morehouse Cummings; "in Just—," copyright 1923, 1951 by E. E. Cummings; "one winter afternoon," copyright © 1960 by E. E. Cummings; "sweet spring is your,"

*For Six Sons
and a
Daughter*

The poems in this anthology are some we have collected while teaching young college students, many of whom have confessed that they didn't like poetry or have protested that they hated having to analyze poems for their "deep hidden meanings." We were dismayed that so many young people should steer themselves away from all poetry just because some poems are like icebergs—with much of their meaning submerged. We wanted them to discover that many poems might give them pleasure, either because the poets had expressed familiar or half-recognized feelings more surely and skillfully than the readers could themselves, or because the poems suggested new and strange ways of looking at the world around them. Therefore, we began a long, rewarding search for poems that would interest our students and other young people and that would speak to them in language that is contemporary and evocative.

The result is a collection of poems that we enjoy and hope others will enjoy, too. They are poems that appeal strongly to the senses, poems that catch the ear whether they are written in meter or free verse, poems that speak about the feelings we all share as we are growing up and even after we are grown. While we have limited our choice to modern poems—most of them written in the last fifteen or twenty years—we have tried not to be merely topical or to express chiefly the frustrations and bitterness of these decades. Even at the worst of times there are moments of wonder, love, joy, humor—moments when we take pleasure in an object closely observed or in the lilt of a song.

We started collecting any poems that we thought were good, short, and lyrical. As we arranged them, we began to see how the poems within a group set each other off, how a group itself changed with the inclusion or exclusion of a particular poem and became something more than the sum of the poems within it. Even the order of arrangement made a difference. But it is not at all necessary to read all the poems in sequence. We expect readers to sample, looking for poems that serve them at the moment, and hope that even the casual reader will find many poems that he likes and will continue to like after living with them for a while. For those who do eventually read straight through, however, we think there is an added pleasure in reading all the poems of a group in order, and the book from beginning to end, letting the poems resonate against each other in the mind.

Helen Hill and Agnes Perkins

CONTENTS

ACKNOWLEDGMENTS, V

FOREWORD, XV

Of Song and Dance, 1

Balance and Skill, 17

Looking at People, 29

Listening to People, 47

Still Lifes and Moving Pictures, 63

The Swift Seasons Roll, 81

With a Hey, Ho, the Wind and the Rain, 112

Father of the Man, 131

When I Was a Child, 149

A Beautiful Brief Moment, 167

A Kiss for Eve, 179

The Buzzing Doubt, 201

Taking Wing, 217

That Dark Other Mountain, 231

Nightmares, 249

INDEX OF POETS, 273

INDEX OF TITLES, 275

INDEX OF FIRST LINES, 279

"And instantly an enormous sanity and hope of strong exultant joy surged up in me again. . . . I knew I should see light once more and know new coasts and come into strange harbors, and see again, as I had once, new lands and morning."

THOMAS WOLFE,
From Death to Morning

Of
Song
and
Dance

Song

Morning opened
Like a rose,
And the snow on the roof
Rose-color took.
Oh, how the street
Toward light did leap!
And the lamps went out.
Brightness fell down
From the steeple clock
To the row of shops
And rippled the bricks
Like the scales of a fish,
And all that day
Was a fairy tale
Told once in a while
To a good child.

DONALD JUSTICE

The Round

Skunk cabbage, bloodroot,
ginseng, spring beauty,
Dutchman's-breeches,
rue, and betony;

bluets, columbine,
cowslip and bittercress,
heartleaf, anemone,
lupin, arbutus;

bunchberry, merrybells,
Jack-in-the-pulpit,
hepatica, vetch,
and dogtooth violet;

pussy-willow, starwort,
wet-dog, trillium,
alumroot, lady's-slipper,
Solomon's plume;

milkweed, fireweed,
loosestrife and dogbane,
sunbright, buttercup,
thistle, and pipevine;

paintbrush, bunchlily,
chicory, candy-root,
spatterdock, sundew,
touch-me-not;

goldenrod, aster,
burdock and coral-
root, gentian, ragweed,
jumpseed, and sorrel;

upland yellow-eye
and Joe-pye-weed,
bittersweet, sumac,
snow, and frozen seed.

PHILIP BOOTH

Sing a Song of Juniper

Sing a song of juniper
Whose song is seldom sung,
Whose needles prick the finger,
Whose berries burn the tongue.

Sing a song of juniper
With boughs shaped like a bowl
For holding sun or snowfall
High on the pasture knoll.

Sing a song of juniper
Whose green is more than green,
Is blue and bronze and violet
And colors in between.

Sing a song of juniper
That keeps close to the ground,
A song composed of silence
And very little sound.

Sing a song of juniper
That hides the hunted mouse,
And gives me outdoor shadows
To haunt my indoor house.

ROBERT FRANCIS

Good Times

My Daddy has paid the rent
and the insurance man is gone
and the lights is back on
and my uncle Brud has hit
for one dollar straight
and they is good times
good times
good times

My Mama has made bread
and Grampaw has come
and everybody is drunk
and dancing in the kitchen
and singing in the kitchen
oh these is good times
good times
good times

oh children think about the
good times

LUCILLE CLIFTON

Serenade

The tin-type tune the locusts make,
Scarlatti-like, among the green
enameled grasses, plucking lutes
of parchment wing with plectrum leg,
ticks off in tones itinerant lives,
and tells in tryst-inviting trills
how love, in miniature modes
and minor forms, perpetuates
the constant, shapely themes of things,
and on melodic clocks records
a transient, true, and treasured bliss.

DOROTHY DONNELLY

First Song

Then it was dusk in Illinois, the small boy
After an afternoon of carting dung
Hung on the rail fence, a sapped thing
Weary to crying. Dark was growing tall
And he began to hear the pond frogs all
Calling upon his ear with what seemed their joy.

Soon their sound was pleasant for a boy
Listening in the smoky dusk and the nightfall
Of Illinois, and then from the field two small
Boys came bearing cornstalk violins
And rubbed three cornstalk bows with resins,
And they sat fiddling with them as with joy.

It was now fine music the frogs and the boys
Did in the towering Illinois twilight make
And into dark in spite of a right arm's ache
A boy's hunched body loved out of a stalk
The first song of his happiness, and the song woke
His heart to the darkness and into the sadness of joy.

GALWAY KINNELL

The Given Note

On the most westerly Blasket
In a dry-stone hut
He got this air out of the night.

Strange noises were heard
By others who followed, bits of a tune
Coming in on loud weather

Though nothing like melody.
He blamed their fingers and ear
As unpractised, their fiddling easy

For he had gone alone into the island
And brought back the whole thing.
The house throbbed like his full violin.

So whether he calls it spirit music
Or not, I don't care. He took it
Out of wind off mid-Atlantic.

Still he maintains, from nowhere.
It comes off the bow gravely,
Rephrases itself into the air.

SEAMUS HEANEY

Song

From whence cometh song?—
From the tear, far away,
From the hound giving tongue,
From the quarry's weak cry.

From whence, love?
From the dirt in the street,
From the bolt, stuck in its groove,
From the cur at my feet.

Whence, death?
From dire hell's mouth,
From the ghost without breath,
The wind shifting south.

THEODORE ROETHKE

buy me an ounce and i'll sell you a pound.
Turn
gert
    (spin!
helen)the
slimmer the finger the thicker the thumb(it's
whirl,
girls)
round and round

early to better is wiser for worse.
Give
liz
   (take!
tommy)we
order a steak and they send us a pie(it's
try,
boys)
mine is yours

ask me the name of the moon in the man.
Up
sam
    (down!
alice)a
hole in the ocean will never be missed(it's
in,
girls)
yours is mine

either was deafer than neither was dumb.
Skip
fred
    (jump!
neddy)but
under the wonder is over the why(it's
now,
boys)
here we come

E. E. CUMMINGS

My Papa's Waltz

The whiskey on your breath
Could make a small boy dizzy;
But I hung on like death:
Such waltzing was not easy.

We romped until the pans
Slid from the kitchen shelf;
My mother's countenance
Could not unfrown itself.

The hand that held my wrist
Was battered on one knuckle;
At every step you missed
My right ear scraped a buckle.

You beat time on my head
With a palm caked hard by dirt,
Then waltzed me off to bed
Still clinging to your shirt.

THEODORE ROETHKE

The Dance

In Breughel's great picture, The Kermess,
the dancers go round, they go round and
around, the squeal and the blare and the
tweedle of bagpipes, a bugle and fiddles
tipping their bellies (round as the thick-
sided glasses whose wash they impound)
their hips and their bellies off balance
to turn them. Kicking and rolling about
the Fair Grounds, swinging their butts, those
shanks must be sound to bear up under such
rollicking measures, prance as they dance
in Breughel's great picture, The Kermess.

WILLIAM CARLOS WILLIAMS

O Daedalus, Fly Away Home

Drifting night in the Georgia pines,
coonskin drum and jubilee banjo.
    Pretty Malinda, dance with me.

Night is juba, night is conjo,
    Pretty Malinda, dance with me.

Night is an African juju man
weaving a wish and a weariness together
    to make two wings.

    O fly away home fly away

Do you remember Africa?

    O cleave the air fly away home

My gran, he flew back to Africa,
just spread his arms and
    flew away home.

Drifting night in the windy pines;
night is a laughing, night is a longing.
    Pretty Malinda, come to me.

Night is a mourning juju man
weaving a wish and a weariness together
    to make two wings.

    O fly away home fly away

ROBERT HAYDEN

Balance
and
Skill

Stabilities

Gull, ballast of its wings.
Word, mind's stone.
Child, love's flesh and bone.

ANNE STEVENSON

Skier

He swings down like the flourish of a pen
Signing a signature in white on white.

The silence of his skis reciprocates
The silence of the world around him.

Wind is his one competitor
In the cool winding and unwinding down.

On incandescent feet he falls
Unfalling, trailing white foam, white fire.

ROBERT FRANCIS

Tightrope Walker

High on the thrilling strand he dances
Laved in white light. The smudged chalk faces
Blur below. His movements scorn
And fluently insult the law
That lumps us, munching, on our seats,
Avoiding the question that slyly tweaks:
How much do we want to see him fall?
It's no use saying we don't at all.
We all know that we hate his breed.
Prancing the nimble thread he's freed
From what we are and gravity.
And yet we know quite well that he
Started just as we began,
That he is, just like us, a man.
(We don't fall off our seats until
We've drunk too much or are feeling ill)
But he has trained the common skill,
Trained and practised; now tonight
It flogs our credence as high and white
In the spotlight's talcum he pirouettes,
Lonely, scorning safety nets,
The highly extraordinary man.
But soon, quite softly, boredom starts
Its muffled drilling at our hearts;
A frisson of coughs and shuffles moves
Over the crowd like a wind through leaves.
Our eyes slide down the air and walk
Idly round the tent as talk
Hums on denial's monotone.
It's just as well the act ends soon
Or we would leave, though not stampede,
Leave furtively in twos and threes,
Absence flooding the canvas house
Where he, alone, all unaware
Would go dancing on the almost air
Till fatigue or error dragged him down,
An ordinary man on ordinary ground.

VERNON SCANNELL

Juggler

A ball will bounce, but less and less. It's not
A light-hearted thing, resents its own resilience.
Falling is what it loves, and the earth falls
So in our hearts from brilliance,
Settles and is forgot.
It takes a sky-blue juggler with five red balls

To shake our gravity up. Whee, in the air
The balls roll round, wheel on his wheeling hands,
Learning the ways of lightness, alter to spheres
Grazing his finger ends,
Cling to their courses there,
Swinging a small heaven about his ears.

But a heaven is easier made of nothing at all
Than the earth regained, and still and sole within
The spin of worlds, with a gesture sure and noble
He reels that heaven in,
Landing it ball by ball,
And trades it all for a broom, a plate, a table.

Oh, on his toes the table is turning, the broom's
Balancing up on his nose, and the plate swirls
On the tip of the broom! Damn, what a show, we cry:
The boys stamp, and the girls
Shriek, and the drum booms
And all comes down, and he bows and says good-bye.

If the juggler is tired now, if the broom stands
In the dust again, if the table starts to drop
Through the daily dark again, and though the plate
Lies flat on the table top,
For him we batter our hands
Who has won for once over the world's weight.

RICHARD WILBUR

Of Kings and Things

What happened to Joey on our block
Who could hit a spaldeen four sewers
And wore his invisible crown
With easy grace, leaning, body-haloed
In the street-lamp night?

He was better than Babe Ruth
Because we could actually see him hit
Every Saturday morning,
With a mop handle thinner than any baseball bat,
That small ball which flew forever.
Whack! straight out at first, then
Rising, rising unbelievably soaring in a
Tremendous heart-bursting trajectory
To come down finally, blocks away,
Bouncing off a parked car's
Fender, eluding the lone outfielder.

Did he get a good job?
Is he married now, with kids?
Is he famous in another constellation?
I saw him with my own eyes in those days
The God of stickball
Disappearing down the street
Skinny and shining in the nightfall light.

LILLIAN MORRISON

The Base Stealer

Poised between going on and back, pulled
Both ways taut like a tightrope-walker,
Fingertips pointing the opposites,
Now bouncing tiptoe like a dropped ball
Or a kid skipping rope, come on, come on,
Running a scattering of steps sidewise,
How he teeters, skitters, tingles, teases,
Taunts them, hovers like an ecstatic bird,
He's only flirting, crowd him, crowd him,
Delicate, delicate, delicate, delicate—now!

ROBERT FRANCIS

Little-League Baseball Fan

No closer the glove clings to the sweaty hand
Than clings my drybones heart
To the being of greenbones there where he jumps and hollers
For the batter to get a hit;
Then comes himself to the proof, the plate, holding
The long bat heavy
And strong to reverse the flight of the whirling, humming
Pitch: sock it like hell.

Lord knows what kind of mystery puts together
Into one flesh the two
Of drybones and greenbones. Yet his every twitch,
Every glint of triumph
At having mastered the ball's trajectory
Is mine, mine too.
I am warm, thoughtless, grinning in the twilight;
My flesh glows, and I thrill.

So be it. For maybe a glow of flesh will cancel
A cold vision clutched
Under the flesh, in my long bones' cells:
Every-man Me confronting
(Unwilling batter) in a game that will not continue
Many more outs, the crossfire
Of the daily sun. And my God, who could connect
With those impossible curves?

W. R. MOSES

Catch

Two boys uncoached are tossing a poem together,
Overhand, underhand, backhand, sleight of hand, every hand,
Teasing with attitudes, latitudes, interludes, altitudes,
High, make him fly off the ground for it, low, make him stoop,
Make him scoop it up, make him as-almost-as-possible miss it,
Fast, let him sting from it, now, now fool him slowly,
Anything, everything tricky, risky, nonchalant,
Anything under the sun to outwit the prosy,
Over the tree and the long sweet cadence down,
Over his head, make him scramble to pick up the meaning,
And now, like a posy, a pretty one plump in his hands.

ROBERT FRANCIS

Mind

Mind in its purest play is like some bat
That beats about in caverns all alone,
Contriving by a kind of senseless wit
Not to conclude against a wall of stone.

It has no need to falter or explore;
Darkly it knows what obstacles are there,
And so may weave and flitter, dip and soar
In perfect courses through the blackest air.

And has this simile a like perfection?
The mind is like a bat. Precisely. Save
That in the very happiest intellection
A graceful error may correct the cave.

RICHARD WILBUR

Looking
at
People

After Snow

GRAZ, AUSTRIA

After snow a lady is out in our garden
Cleaning the trees.
She carries a long, light pole.
First she rattles the bamboo
And the low bushy still-green plants.
Now she is chastising a fir tree,
Now the ivy along the wall.
She has covered her footprints
With helpings of snow.

And now she has gone.

WALTER CLARK

one winter afternoon

(at the magical hour
when is becomes if)

a bespangled clown
standing on eighth street
handed me a flower.

Nobody,it's safe
to say,observed him but

myself;and why?because

without any doubt he was
whatever(first and last)

mostpeople fear most:
a mystery for which i've
no word except alive

—that is,completely alert
and miraculously whole;

with not merely a mind and a heart

but unquestionably a soul—
by no means funereally hilarious

(or otherwise democratic)
but essentially poetic
or ethereally serious:

a fine not a coarse clown
(no mob,but a person)

and while never saying a word

who was anything but dumb;
since the silence of him

self sang like a bird.
Mostpeople have been heard
screaming for international

measures that render hell rational
—i thank heaven somebody's crazy

enough to give me a daisy

E. E. CUMMINGS

The Grandfathers

Why will they never sleep?
                —JOHN PEALE BISHOP

Why will they never speak,
The old ones, the grandfathers?
Always you find them sitting
On ruined porches, deep
In the back country, at dusk,
Hawking and spitting.
They might have sat there forever,
Tapping their sticks,
Peevish, discredited gods.
Ask of the traveler how,
At road end, they will fix
You maybe with the cold
Eye of a snake or a bird
And answer not a word,
Only these blank, oracular
Headshakes or headnods.

DONALD JUSTICE

Kid

CUERNAVACA

He is found with the homeless dogs
    that worry sidewalk cafes
where gringos in dollar bills
    deplore and sip. He has

Tricks of pathos for
    the silly foreigners
and so manages not to starve.
    Waiters strike at him and curse;

Deft and quick and accustomed,
    he dances beyond their blows,
taunts them and scampers off,
    laughing as he goes.

ROBERT HAYDEN

Niño Leading an Old Man to Market

He is leading his grandfather under the sun to market.
Who needs to see? The hand is warm on his shoulder.
The sun tells a man whatever he has to know
And the eyes of the children take care of the rest.

This is a little procession, solemn and steady,
A way of seeing that has the right direction,
And needs the simplest of eyes; the hand is quite sure,
And the wealth of the sun takes care of the rest.

His children have children to spare for any errand
An old man must go on; like sun, they are warmly with him,
Though at night his wakeful hand may remember that seeing
Was going alone in any direction.

Time takes care of the rest. In the niño's eyes
He is leading his grandfather under the sun to market.
In the old man's mind he walks through warmth where he must.
They are going in one direction, and know it.

LEONARD NATHAN

Ben

My Brother Ben's face, thought Eugene,
Is like a piece of slightly yellow ivory;
His high white head is knotted fiercely
By his old man's scowl;
His mouth is like a knife,
His smile the flicker of light across a blade.
His face is like a blade, and a knife,
And a flicker of light:
It is delicate and fierce,
And scowls beautifully forever,
And when he fastens his hard white fingers
And his scowling eyes
Upon a thing he wants to fix,
He sniffs
With sharp and private concentration
Through his long pointed nose.
Thus women, looking, feel a well of tenderness
For his pointed, bumpy, always scowling face:
His hair shines like that of a young boy—
It is crinkled and crisp as lettuce.

THOMAS WOLFE

House Guest

The sad seamstress
who stays with us this month
is small and thin and bitter.
No one can cheer her up.
Give her a dress, a drink,
roast chicken, or fried fish—
it's all the same to her.

She sits and watches TV.
No, she watches zigzags.
"Can you adjust the TV?"
"No," she says. No hope.
She watches on and on,
without hope, without air.

Her own clothes give us pause,
but she's not a poor orphan.
She has a father, a mother,
and all that, and she's earning
quite well, and we're stuffing
her with fattening foods.

We invite her to use the binoculars.
We say, "Come see the jets!"
We say, "Come see the baby!"
Or the knife grinder who cleverly
plays the National Anthem
on his wheel so shrilly.
Nothing helps.

She speaks: "I need a little
money to buy buttons."
She seems to think it's useless
to ask. Heavens, buy buttons,
if they'll do any good,
the biggest in the world—
by the dozen, by the gross!
Buy yourself an ice cream,
a comic book, a cat!

Her face is closed as a nut,
closed as a careful snail
or a thousand-year-old seed.
Does she dream of marriage?
Of getting rich? Her sewing
is decidedly mediocre.

Please! Take our money! Smile!
What on earth have we done?
What has everyone done
and when did it all begin?
Then one day she confides
that she wanted to be a nun
and her family opposed her.

Perhaps we should let her go,
or deliver her straight off
to the nearest convent—and wasn't
her month up last week, anyway?

Can it be that we nourish
one of the Fates in our bosoms?
Clotho, sewing our lives
with a bony little foot
on a borrowed sewing machine,
and our fates will be like hers,
and our hems crooked forever?

                    ELIZABETH BISHOP

Snapshots of a Daughter-in-law

PART I

You, once a belle in Shreveport,
with henna-colored hair, skin like a peachbud,
still have your dresses copied from that time,
and play a Chopin prelude
called by Cortot: "Delicious recollections
float like perfume through the memory."

Your mind now, mouldering like wedding-cake,
heavy with useless experience, rich
with suspicion, rumor, fantasy,
crumbling to pieces under the knife-edge
of mere fact. In the prime of your life.

Nervy, glowering, your daughter
wipes the teaspoons, grows another way.

ADRIENNE RICH

Woman with Girdle

Your midriff sags toward your knees;
your breasts lie down in air,
their nipples as uninvolved
as warm starfish.
You stand in your elastic case,
still not giving up the new-born
and the old-born cycle.
Moving, you roll down the garment,
down that pink snapper and hoarder,
as your belly, soft as pudding,
slops into the empty space;
down, over the surgeon's careful mark,
down over hips, those head cushions
and mouth cushions,
slow motion like a rolling pin,
over crisp hairs, that amazing field
that hides your genius from your patron;
over thighs, thick as young pigs,
over knees like saucers,
over calves, polished as leather,
down toward the feet.
You pause for a moment,
tying your ankles into knots.
Now you rise,
a city from the sea,
born long before Alexandria was,
straightway from God you have come
into your redeeming skin.

ANNE SEXTON

40

On Hurricane Jackson

Now his nose's bridge is broken, one eye
will not focus and the other is a stray;
trainers whisper in his mouth while one ear
listens to itself, clenched like a fist;
generally shadow-boxing in a smoky room,
his mind hides like the aching boys
who lost a contest in the Pan-Hellenic games
and had to take the back roads home,
but someone else, his perfect youth,
laureled in newsprint and dollar bills,
triumphs forever on the great white way
to the statistical Sparta of the champs.

ALAN DUGAN

Elegy

Her face like a rain-beaten stone on the day she rolled off
With the dark hearse, and enough flowers for an alderman—
And so she was, in her way, Aunt Tilly.

Sighs, sighs, who says they have sequence?
Between the spirit and the flesh—what war?
She never knew;
For she asked no quarter and gave none,
Who sat with the dead when the relatives left,
Who fed and tended the infirm, the mad, the epileptic,
And, with a harsh rasp of a laugh at herself,
Faced up to the worst.

I recall how she harried the children away all the late summer
From the one beautiful thing in her yard, the peach tree;
How she kept the wizened, the fallen, the misshapen for herself,
And picked and pickled the best, to be left on rickety doorsteps.

And yet she died in agony,
Her tongue, at the last, thick, black as an oxen's.

Terror of cops, bill collectors, betrayers of the poor,—
I see you in some celestial supermarket
Moving serenely among the leeks and cabbages,
Probing the squash,
Bearing down, with two steady eyes,
On the quaking butcher.

THEODORE ROETHKE

To My Mother

Most near, most dear, most loved and most far,
Under the window where I often found her
Sitting as huge as Asia, seismic with laughter,
Gin and chicken helpless in her Irish hand,
Irresistible as Rabelais, but most tender for
The lame dogs and hurt birds that surround her,—
She is a procession no one can follow after
But be like a little dog following a brass band.

She will not glance up at the bomber, or condescend
To drop her gin and scuttle to a cellar,
But lean on the mahogany table like a mountain
Whom only faith can move, and so I send
O all my faith, and all my love to tell her
That she will move from mourning into morning.

GEORGE BARKER

Old Florist

That hump of a man bunching chrysanthemums
Or pinching-back asters, or planting azaleas,
Tamping and stamping dirt into pots,—
How he could flick and pick
Rotten leaves or yellowy petals,
Or scoop out a weed close to flourishing roots,
Or make the dust buzz with a light spray,
Or drown a bug in one spit of tobacco juice,
Or fan life into wilted sweet-peas with his hat,
Or stand all night watering roses, his feet blue in rubber boots.

THEODORE ROETHKE

He Was

a brown old man with a green thumb:
I can remember the screak on stones of his hoe,
The chug, choke, and high madrigal wheeze
Of the spray-cart bumping below
The sputtery leaves of the apple trees,
But he was all but dumb

Who filled some quarter of the day with sound
All of my childhood long. For all I heard
Of all his labors, I can now recall
Never a single word
Until he went in the dead of fall
To the drowsy underground,

Having planted a young orchard with so great care
In that last year that none was lost, and May
Aroused them all, the leaves saying the land's
Praise for the livening clay,
And the found voice of his buried hands
Rose in the sparrowy air.

RICHARD WILBUR

"How Long Hast Thou Been a Gravemaker?"

FOR E. S. GRANT, BURIED IN MONTANA

Shakespeare would have savored his coarse, irate
Damnation of weakness, his heroic stance,
Arthritic in arms and legs as well as hands,
As he held, in balance, ready to pitch, the weight
Of a shovelful of gravel. Dawn till dark,
Picking and shoveling slowly, working his way
Down to the level of his blue eyes in clay,
He lived with a curious joy, where the meadowlark
Nested and fluted near his deepening pit.
He spurned all help, alone with the prairie wind.
One day, exhausted, he took a renewing swig
From a jug of shade-cool water, rested a bit,
Hobbled among old gravestones, chuckled and grinned,
And picked his own spot, for somebody else to dig.

DAVID PERKINS

45

Listening
to
People

A *Time to Talk*

When a friend calls to me from the road
And slows his horse to a meaning walk,
I don't stand still and look around
On all the hills I haven't hoed,
And shout from where I am, "What is it?"
No, not as there is a time to talk.
I thrust my hoe in the mellow ground,
Blade-end up and five feet tall,
And plod: I go up to the stone wall
For a friendly visit.

ROBERT FROST

Romping

Silly. All giggles and ringlets and never
about to stop anything without fussing:
get down I say! Do you think I took your mother
to beget me a chimp for my shoulder?
I'm forty, boy, and no weight lifter.
Go find some energy your own size.
Get down!—Well, just once more.
There. Now get down, you baby-fat incubus.
Go ride your imagination. No, I don't care
how many kisses you'll write me a check for.
A million? Some banker you are. Still—
a million of anything is a lot of something.
All right. Once more, then. But just once. You hear?

JOHN CIARDI

To Theon from his son Theon

TUBI 18, 2ND CENTURY A.D.

"Theon to his father Theon greetings. Another
Fine thing, father, not to take me to town.
I will not write, or speak, or settle down
Unless you bring me to Alexandria. Mother
Said to Archelaus: 'I can't tell
You how he upsets me. Take him away.'
I beg you, send for me. Until that day
I will not eat, or drink. There now. Farewell."
This voice, charged with a child's longing, a child's rage,
Called eighteen centuries ago
From the sands where the paper-trees grow.
There is an Alexandria for every age.

C. A. TRYPANIS

Lizards and Snakes

On the summer road that ran by our front porch
    Lizards and snakes came out to sun.
It was hot as a stove out there, enough to scorch
    A buzzard's foot. Still, it was fun
To lie in the dust and spy on them. Near but remote,
    They snoozed in the carriage ruts, a smile
In the set of the jaw, a fierce pulse in the throat
Working away like Jack Doyle's after he's run the mile.

Aunt Martha had an unfair prejudice
    Against them (as well as being cold
Toward bats). She was pretty inflexible in this,
    Being a spinster and all, and old.
So we used to slip them into her knitting box.
    In the evening she'd bring in things to mend
And a nice surprise would slide out from under the socks.
It broadened her life, as Joe said. Joe was my friend.

But we never did it again after the day
    Of the big wind when you could hear the trees
Creak like rockingchairs. She was looking away
    Off, and kept saying, "Sweet Jesus, please
Don't let him near me. He's as like as twins.
    He can crack us like lice with his fingernail.
I can see him plain as a pikestaff. Look how he grins
And swinges the scaly horror of his folded tail."

ANTHONY HECHT

The High School Band

On warm days in September the high school band
Is up with the birds and marches along our street,
Boom, boom,
To a field where it goes boom boom until eight forty-five
When it marches, as in the old rhyme, back, boom boom,
To its study halls, leaving our street
Empty except for the leaves that descend, to no drum,
And lie still.
In September
A great many high school bands beat a great many drums,
And the silences after their partings are very deep.

REED WHITTEMORE

Reason

Said, Pull her up a bit will you, Mac, I want to unload there.
Said, Pull her up my rear end, first come first serve.
Said, Give her the gun, Bud, he needs a taste of his own bumper.

Then the usher came out and got into the act:
Said, Pull her up, pull her up a bit, we need this space, sir.
Said, For God's sake, is this still a free country or what?
You go back and take care of Gary Cooper's horse
And leave me handle my own car.

Saw them unloading the lame old lady,
Ducked out under the wheel and gave her an elbow,
Said, All you needed to do was just explain;
Reason, Reason is my middle name.

JOSEPHINE MILES

54

Cora Punctuated with Strawberries

Sandra and that boy that's going to get her in trouble
one of these days were out in the garden where anyone in
Mother's sickroom could see them out the upperleft corner of the
window sitting behind the garage feeding each other
blueberries and Cherry was helping with the dishes alone in the
kitchen and
um good strawberries if we did grow them just can't can without
popping one in every so often Henry was at it again in the
attic with that whatchamacallit of his when the Big
Bomb fell smack in the MacDonalds' yard you know over on
Elm and they got into Life and the papers and all all very
well but they might have been in when it hit and it would have
been a very different story for Lucy MacDonald then I'll tell
you well they say it was right in the Geographic Center of the
country the Geographic
woody Center you could hear it just as plain I thought the
elevator had blown up and I guess you read yourself the awful
things it would have
ak another one woody I tell you I don't know what's got
into these strawberries used to be so juicy they
say they only had one and it's all it would have took well I
always knew we could beat the enemy they made such
shoddy tricks and spring-toys and puzzles and fuses and
things and besides, it wouldn't have been right.

GEORGE STARBUCK

A Teacher

He hated them all one by one but wanted to show them
What was Important and Vital and by God if
They thought they'd never have use for it he was
Sorry as hell for them that's all, with their genteel
Mercantile Main Street Babbitt
Bourgeois-barbaric faces, they were beyond
Saving, clearly, quite out of reach, and so he
G-rrr
Got up every morning and g-rrr ate his breakfast
And g-rrr lumbered off to his eight o'clock
Gladly to teach.

REED WHITTEMORE

"next to of course god america i
love you land of the pilgrims' and so forth oh
say can you see by the dawn's early my
country 'tis of centuries come and go
and are no more what of it we should worry
in every language even deafanddumb
thy sons acclaim your glorious name by gorry
by jingo by gee by gosh by gum
why talk of beauty what could be more beautiful than these heroic happy dead
who rushed like lions to the roaring slaughter
they did not stop to think they died instead
then shall the voice of liberty be mute?"

He spoke.   And drank rapidly a glass of water

E. E. CUMMINGS

A Glass of Beer

The lanky hank of a she in the inn over there
Nearly killed me for asking the loan of a glass of beer;
May the devil grip the whey-faced slut by the hair,
And beat bad manners out of her skin for a year.

That parboiled ape, with the toughest jaw you will see
On virtue's path, and a voice that would rasp the dead,
Came roaring and raging the minute she looked at me,
And threw me out of the house on the back of my head!

If I asked her master he'd give me a cask a day;
But she, with the beer at hand, not a gill would arrange!
May she marry a ghost and bear him a kitten, and may
The High King of Glory permit her to get the mange.

JAMES STEPHENS

Traveller's Curse After Misdirection

FROM THE WELSH

May they stumble, stage by stage
On an endless pilgrimage,
Dawn and dusk, mile after mile
At each and every step a stile;
At each and every step withal
May they catch their feet and fall;
At each and every fall they take
May a bone within them break;
And may the bone that breaks within
Not be, for variation's sake,
Now rib, now thigh, now arm, now shin,
But always, without fail, THE NECK.

ROBERT GRAVES

Uncle Death

Was I surprised!
Uncle Death stepped out of the wood
All of a sudden
Like Rip Van Winkle
Smelling of
Leaves and mud.

He had the family eyes.

"Give over ploughing," he said.
"It's been a long time,"
Slitting a straw,
"Are there children?" he said.

"Two boys and a girl.
Will you be long?"
"Only tonight.
Gone by tomorrow."
"I'll tell Mary
To make up the bed."

"No need," he said.

WALTER CLARK

Still
Lifes
and
Moving
Pictures

A Talisman

Under a splintered mast,
Torn from the ship and cast
    Near her hull,

A stumbling shepherd found
Embedded in the ground,
    A seagull

Of lapislazuli,
A scarab of the sea,
    With wings spread—

Curling its coral feet,
Parting its beak to greet
    Men long dead.

MARIANNE MOORE

Manhole Covers

The beauty of manhole covers—what of that?
Like medals struck by a great savage khan,
Like Mayan calendar stones, unliftable, indecipherable,
Not like old electrum, chased and scored,
Mottoed and sculptured to a turn,
But notched and whelked and pocked and smashed
With the great company names:
Gentle Bethlehem, smiling United States.
This rustproof artifact of my street,
Long after roads are melted away, will lie
Sidewise in the graves of the iron-old world,
Bitten at the edges,
Strong with its cryptic American,
Its dated beauty.

KARL SHAPIRO

Utah

Somewhere nowhere in Utah, a boy by the roadside,
gun in his hand, and the rare dumb hard tears flowing.
Beside him, the greyheaded man has let one arm slide
awkwardly over his shoulders, is talking and pointing
at whatever it is, dead, in the dust on the ground.

By the old parked Chevy, two women, talking and watching.
Their skirts flag forward; bandannas twist with their hair.
Around them some sheep and a fence and the sagebrush burning
and burning with its grey blue flame. In the distance, somewhere
where the mountains are clouds, lightning, but no rain.

ANNE STEVENSON

Sitting in the Woods: A Contemplation

I

Here am I, a shape under a cedar,
And all the world takes bearings on the shape.
An oak-sitting squirrel, wary for quick escape,

Yet pins me with his eye. A jittery wren,
Though he clings to his skinny twig upside down,
Pins me. Under my back and legs, the brown

Cedar needles record exactly a weight;
Over my face and belly and hands, the warm,
Cedary air records exactly a form.

Every leaf on certain thousands of twigs,
Each stone nearby, and berry and haw and hip
Notes that there is exact relationship

Of degree, minute, and second, on a certain plain,
Between itself and the shape I thought was free,
Sprawled in the woods under a cedar tree.

II

That giant Gulliver was not so bound
By all those cables the little men drew tight
As I by this amazing cobweb of right

Records and measurements. Now, can one center
A web like this, with the number of strands so great,
And then, by his single will and his single weight,

Break loose? Will it not be a complaisant ghost
That smiles tonight in the room where I should appear,
While I stay under the cedar, fixed here?

W. R. MOSES

The Farm

FOR NINA AND VAL

Where peace goes whispering by,
creaks in the turning windmill,
lows in the cattle;
where the hot light stretches over the fields
like a lazy cat;
where the clouds scatter
and graze like sheep on the barren skies,
but gather no rain;
where the darkness opens its fist
spilling stars and the wind;
where love has grown quiet,
assuming the shapes
of the soil and the rock and the tree—
here in this land
let me rest, rest, rest, oh, filling my heart
full of a sweet emptiness!

VASSAR MILLER

Dingman's Marsh

Anywhere I look
the water has dominion, has drawn itself
against the birches until they die
and dying make a mat of tangled limbs
between the darker firs and pines.
But birds,
hell-divers, all the ducks, bitterns and herons
flourish and mark the dark waters
with their going, ferries to wherever.
Or the muskrats in their wet houses,
coming out to swim snout up under a falling sky.

This is a happy doom, a place of happy ends
where water can creep as it will
and sodden the grasses,
last year's blackberry bushes.
In the white sky over all this place
the marsh hawks float on another water,
made fragile in the failing light.

JOHN MOORE

Cat on Couch

My cat, washing her tail's tip, is a whorl
Of white shell,
As perfect as a fan
In full half-moon . . . Next moment she's a hare:
The muzzle softens, rounds, goes dumb, and one
Tall ear dips, falters forward . . . Then,
Cross as switches, she's a great horned owl;
Two leafy tricorned ears reverse, a frown
Darkens her chalky visage, big eyes round
And round and stare down midnight.
                               There sits my cat
Mysterious as gauze,—now somnolent,
Now jocose, quicksilver from a dropped
Thermometer. When poised
Below the sketched ballet-
Dancers who pirouette upon the wall,
Calmly she lifts the slim
Boom of her leg, what will
The prima ballerina next
Perform?—Grace held in readiness,
She meditates, a vision of repose.

BARBARA HOWES

Lobsters in the Window

First, you think they are dead.
Then you are almost sure
One is beginning to stir.
Out of the crushed ice, slow
As the hands of a schoolroom clock,
He lifts his one great claw
And holds it over his head;
Now, he is trying to walk.

But like a run-down toy;
Like the backward crabs we boys
Splashed after in the creek,
Trapped in jars or a net,
And then took home to keep.
Overgrown, retarded, weak,
He is fumbling yet
From the deep chill of his sleep

As if, in a glacial thaw,
Some ancient thing might wake
Sore and cold and stiff
Struggling to raise one claw
Like a defiant fist;
Yet wavering, as if
Starting to swell and ache
With that thick peg in the wrist.

I should wave back, I guess.
But still in his permanent clench
He's fallen back with the mass
Heaped in their common trench
Who stir, but do not look out
Through the rainstreaming glass,
Hear what the newsboys shout,
Or see the raincoats pass.

W. D. SNODGRASS

Washing Windows

FOR LAURA AND HERB JACKSON

On a ladder, in an old checkered shirt,
he takes the rag she offers from within.
Their hands begin
slowly to circle, polishing,
and for a time, as particles
on a field of force align,
their hands move one to one,
tight, in a dance, and the glass goes bright
between them, hard, a clearing lens.
They pause and smile, at peace,
each in his own condition.

BARRY SPACKS

Driving Toward
the Lac Qui Parle River

I

I am driving; it is dusk; Minnesota.
The stubble field catches the last growth of sun.
The soybeans are breathing on all sides.
Old men are sitting before their houses on carseats
In the small towns. I am happy,
The moon rising above the turkey sheds.

II

The small world of the car
Plunges through the deep fields of the night,
On the road from Willmar to Milan.
This solitude covered with iron
Moves through the fields of night
Penetrated by the noise of crickets.

III

Nearly to Milan, suddenly a small bridge,
And water kneeling in the moonlight.
In small towns the houses are built right on the ground;
The lamplight falls on all fours on the grass.
When I reach the river, the full moon covers it;
A few people are talking low in a boat.

ROBERT BLY

The Sappa Creek

Old rusty-belly thing will soon be gone
Scrap and busted while we're still on earth—
But here you cry for care,
We paint your steel shelves red
& store the big brass valves with green
Wheel handles. Dustpan and wastecan
Nestle in the corner—
Contemplating what to throw away.
Rags in bales, the final home for bathrobes,
Little boy bluejeans and housewife dresses
Gay print splash—all wiping oil off floorplates,
Dangling from hip pockets like a scalp.
Chipping paint, packing valves, going nuts,
Eating frozen meat, we wander greasy nurses
Tending sick and nervous old & cranky ship.

GARY SNYDER

Pancho Villa

"I am Pancho Villa," says the truck
in crude yellow letters painted on its grill
and battles through the traffic armed
with these words—idiotic, gleeful.

Caught, it pivots proud as a dancer
in the storm of cars and buses,
then thrusts on, forcing the autos aside,
boasting, threatening, ignoring the torrents of abuse,

saying, "I am Pancho Villa
the Mexican bandit, the mustachioed one.
Who would contain me? Who would know my measure?
I sweep the valleys like the coming of rain."

So, poor truck, green truck—
one drop in the metropolitan flow.
So, working heart.
So, old truculence—our thundercloud, our rainbow.

LOU LIPSITZ

A Fire-Truck

Right down the shocked street with a siren-blast
That sends all else skittering to the curb,
Redness, brass, ladders and hats hurl past,
    Blurring to sheer verb,

Shift at the corner into uproarious gear
And make it around the turn in a squall of traction,
The headlong bell maintaining sure and clear,
    Thought is degraded action!

Beautiful, heavy, unweary, loud, obvious thing!
I stand here purged of nuance, my mind a blank.
All I was brooding upon has taken wing,
    And I have you to thank.

As you howl beyond hearing I carry you into my mind,
Ladders and brass and all, there to admire
Your phoenix-red simplicity, enshrined
    In that not extinguished fire.

RICHARD WILBUR

A Black November Turkey

TO A.M. AND A.M.

Nine white chickens come
With haunchy walk and heads
Jabbing among the chips, the chaff, the stones
    And the cornhusk-shreds,

And bit by bit infringe
A pond of dusty light,
Spectral in shadow until they bobbingly one
    By one ignite.

Neither pale nor bright,
The turkey-cock parades
Through radiant squalors, darkly auspicious as
    The ace of spades,

Himself his own cortège
And puffed with the pomp of death,
Rehearsing over and over with strangled râle
    His latest breath.

The vast black body floats
Above the crossing knees
As a cloud over thrashed branches, a calm ship
    Over choppy seas,

Shuddering its fan and feathers
In fine soft clashes
With the cold sound that the wind makes, fondling
    Paper-ashes.

The pale-blue bony head
Set on its shepherd's-crook
Like a saint's death-mask, turns a vague, superb
    And timeless look

Upon these clocking hens
And the cocks that one by one,
Dawn after mortal dawn, with vulgar joy
    Acclaim the sun.

RICHARD WILBUR

The Chipmunk's Day

In and out the bushes, up the ivy,
Into the hole
By the old oak stump, the chipmunk flashes.
Up the pole

To the feeder full of seeds he dashes,
Stuffs his cheeks,
The chickadee and titmouse scold him.
Down he streaks.

Red as the leaves the wind blows off the maple,
Red as a fox,
Striped like a skunk, the chipmunk whistles
Past the love seat, past the mailbox,

Down the path,
Home to his warm hole stuffed with sweet
Things to eat.
Neat and slight and shining, his front feet

Curled at his breast, he sits there while the sun
Stripes the red west
With its last light: the chipmunk
Dives to his rest.

RANDALL JARRELL

Hunting Song

The fox he came lolloping, lolloping,
Lolloping. His eyes were bright,
His ears were high.
He was like death at the end of a string
When he came to the hollow
Log. He ran in one side
And out of the other. O
He was sly.

The hounds they came tumbling, tumbling,
Tumbling. Their heads were low,
Their eyes were red.
The sound of their breath was louder than death
When they came to the hollow
Log. They boiled at one end
But a bitch found the scent. O
They were mad.

The hunter came galloping, galloping,
Galloping. All damp was his mare
From her hooves to her mane.
His coat and his mouth were redder than death
When he came to the hollow
Log. He took in the rein
And over he went. O
He was fine.

The log he just lay there, alone in
The clearing. No fox nor hound
Nor mounted man
Saw his black round eyes in their perfect disguise
(As the ends of a hollow
Log). He watched death go through him,
Around him and over him. O
He was wise.

DONALD FINKEL

The
Swift
Seasons
Roll

Spring

First Sight

Lambs that learn to walk in snow
When their bleating clouds the air
Meet a vast unwelcome, know
Nothing but a sunless glare.
Newly stumbling to and fro
All they find, outside the fold,
Is a wretched width of cold.

As they wait beside the ewe,
Her fleeces wetly caked, there lies
Hidden round them, waiting too,
Earth's immeasurable surprise.
They could not grasp it if they knew,
What so soon will wake and grow
Utterly unlike the snow.

PHILIP LARKIN

March

I

Winter is long in this climate
and spring—a matter of a few days
only,—a flower or two picked
from mud or from among wet leaves
or at best against treacherous
bitterness of wind, and sky shining
teasingly, then closing in black
and sudden, with fierce jaws.

WILLIAM CARLOS WILLIAMS

Thaw in the City

Now my legs begin to walk,
The filthy piles of snow are melting.
Pavements are wet.

What clear, tiny streams!
Suddenly I feel the blood flowing in the veins
in the backs of my hands.

And I hear a voice—a wonderful voice—
as if someone I loved had lifted a window
and called my name.

The streets wash over me like waves.
I sail in a boat of factories and sparrows
out of sight.

LOU LIPSITZ

in Just-
spring   when the world is mud-
luscious the little
lame balloonman

whistles   far   and wee

and eddieandbill come
running from marbles and
piracies and it's
spring

when the world is puddle-wonderful

the queer
old balloonman whistles
far   and   wee
and bettyandisbel come dancing

from hop-scotch and jump-rope and

it's
spring
and
    the

        goat-footed

balloonMan   whistles
far
and
wee

E. E. CUMMINGS

And When the Green Man Comes

The man is clothed
in birchbark,
small birds cling to his limbs
and one builds
a nest in his ear.

The clamor of bedlam
infests his hair, a wind
blowing in his head
shakes down
a thought that turns
to moss and lichen
at his feet.

His eyes are blind
with April,
his breath distilled
of butterflies
and bees, and in his beard
the maggot sings.

He comes again
with litter of chips
and empty cans,
his shoes full of mud and dung;

an army of shedding dogs
attends him,
the valley shudders where
he stands,
            redolent of roses,
exalted in
the streaming rain.

JOHN HAINES

That Sharp Knife

Yes,
And in that month when Proserpine comes back,
And Ceres' dead heart rekindles,
When all the woods
Are a tender smoky blur,
And birds no bigger than a budding leaf
Dart through the singing trees,
And when odorous tar comes spongy in the streets,
And boys roll balls of it upon their tongues,
And they are lumpy with tops and agate marbles;
And there is blasting thunder in the night,
And the soaking million-footed rain,
And one looks out at morning on a stormy sky,
A broken wrack of cloud;
And when the mountain boy brings water
To his kinsmen laying fence,
And as the wind snakes through the grasses
Hears far in the valley below
The long wail of the whistle,
And the faint clangor of a bell;
And the blue great cup of the hills
Seems closer, nearer,
For he has heard an inarticulate promise:
He has been pierced by Spring,
That sharp knife.

THOMAS WOLFE

Spring in These Hills

Slow May
deliberate in the peach tree,
lighting the pear blossoms, one first then another,
sullen almost sometimes,
comes,
delicately through the thaws of snow
to scatter
daffodils like drifting flaws
of sunlight on these winter hills.

ARCHIBALD MACLEISH

A Late Spring Day in My Life

A silence hovers over the earth:
The grass lifts lightly in the heat
Like the ancient wing of a bird.
A horse gazes steadily at me.

ROBERT BLY

Seed Leaves

HOMAGE TO R. F.

Here something stubborn comes,
Dislodging the earth crumbs
And making crusty rubble.
It comes up bending double,
And looks like a green staple.
It could be seedling maple,
Or artichoke, or bean.
That remains to be seen.

Forced to make choice of ends,
The stalk in time unbends,
Shakes off the seed-case, heaves
Aloft, and spreads two leaves
Which still display no sure
And special signature.
Toothless and fat, they keep
The oval form of sleep.

This plant would like to grow
And yet be embryo;
Increase, and yet escape
The doom of taking shape;
Be vaguely vast, and climb
To the tip end of time
With all of space to fill,
Like boundless Igdrasil
That has the stars for fruit.

But something at the root
More urgent than that urge
Bids two true leaves emerge,
And now the plant, resigned
To being self-defined
Before it can commerce
With the great universe,
Takes aim at all the sky
And starts to ramify.

RICHARD WILBUR

Summer

Summer Music

Summer is all a green air—
From the brilliant lawn, sopranos
Through murmuring hedges
Accompanied by high poplars;
In fields of wheat, surprises;
Through faraway pastures, flows
In slow decrescendos.

Summer is all a green sound—
Rippling in the foreground
To that soft applause,
The foam of Queen Anne's lace.
Green, green in the ear
Is all we care to hear.
Until a field suddenly flashes
The singing with so sharp
A yellow that it smashes
Loud cymbals in the ear.
Minor has turned to major
As summer, lulling and so mild,
Goes golden-buttercup-wild.

MAY SARTON

My Father Paints the Summer

A smoky rain riddles the ocean plains,
Rings on the beaches' stones, stomps in the swales,
Batters the panes
Of the shore hotel, and the hoped-for summer chills and fails.
The summer people sigh,
"Is this July?"

They talk by the lobby fire but no one hears
For the thrum of the rain. In the dim and sounding halls,
Din at the ears,
Dark at the eyes well in the head, and the ping-pong balls
Scatter their hollow knocks
Like crazy clocks.

But up in his room by artificial light
My father paints the summer, and his brush
Tricks into sight
The prosperous sleep, the girdling stir and clear steep hush
Of a summer never seen,
A granted green.

Summer, luxuriant Sahara, the orchard spray
Gales in the Eden trees, the knight again
Can cast away
His burning mail, Rome is at Anzio: but the rain
For the ping-pong's optative bop
Will never stop.

Caught Summer is always an imagined time.
Time gave it, yes, but time out of any mind.
There must be prime
In the heart to beget that season, to reach past rain and find
Riding the palest days
Its perfect blaze.

RICHARD WILBUR

"Summertime and the living . . ."

Nobody planted roses, he recalls,
but sunflowers gangled there sometimes,
tough-stalked and bold
and like the vivid children there unplanned.
There circus-poster horses curveted
in trees of heaven
above the quarrels and shattered glass,
and he was bareback rider of them all.

No roses there in summer—
oh, never roses except when people died—
and no vacations for his elders,
so harshened after each unrelenting day
that they were shouting-angry.
But summer was, they said, the poor folks' time
of year. And he remembers
how they would sit on broken steps amid

The fevered tossings of the dusk, the dark,
wafting hearsay with funeral-parlor fans
or making evening solemn by
their quietness. Feels their Mosaic eyes
upon him, though the florist roses
that only sorrow could afford
long since have bidden them Godspeed.

Oh, summer summer summertime—

Then grim street preachers shook
their tambourines and Bibles in the face
of tolerant wickedness;
then Elks parades and big splendiferous
Jack Johnson in his diamond limousine
set the ghetto burgeoning
with fantasies
of Ethiopia spreading her gorgeous wings.

ROBERT HAYDEN

Mid-August at Sourdough Mountain Lookout

Down valley a smoke haze
Three days heat, after five days rain
Pitch glows on the fir-cones
Across rocks and meadows
Swarms of new flies.

I cannot remember things I once read
A few friends, but they are in cities.
Drinking cold snow-water from a tin cup
Looking down for miles
Through high still air.

GARY SNYDER

Exeunt

Piecemeal the summer dies;
At the field's edge a daisy lives alone;
A last shawl of burning lies
On a grey field-stone.

All cries are thin and terse;
The field has droned the summer's final mass;
A cricket like a dwindled hearse
Crawls from the dry grass.

RICHARD WILBUR

Autumn

Leaflight

The trees turn:
flower-yellow
on the willow,
red of the rose
on maple boughs;
the sumacs burn.

The leaves fall:
walnut, alder,
poplar, elder,
and elms unveil,
dropping gold foil
on field and wall.

DOROTHY DONNELLY

Indian Summer: Vermont

All through October
the hot leaves shifted,
scratched with their paper
on the iron pastures,
filled with their paper colors
the metallic waterholes.

The air was sweet,
corrupt with incurable fevers,
and the fish died willingly
in the wrinkled scars of the riverbeds.
Wherever a fly was,
there was a death.
Wherever the grass was,
its fine points
splintered with meticulous explosions.

The sun grew larger;
the land withered;
the leopard and salmon
and kite-colored days
disappeared.

And still no hour advanced upon another,
no one wind came to ravage the orchards.
And still, in the end, the leaves dropped.
The branches were nets
constellated with apples.
Then these dropped too.
In the grey desolation
the land was its stones.

ANNE STEVENSON

Field of Autumn

Slow moves the acid breath of noon
over the copper-coated hill,
slow from the wild crabs' bearded breast
the palsied apples fall.

Like coloured smoke the day hangs fire,
taking the village without sound;
the vulture-headed sun lies low
chained to the violet ground.

The horse upon the rocky height
rolls all the valley in his eye,
but dares not raise his foot nor move
his shoulder from the fly.

The sheep, snail-backed against the wall,
lifts her blind face, but does not know
the cry her blackened tongue gives forth
is the first bleat of snow.

Each leaf and stone, each roof and well
feels the gold foot of autumn pass;
each spider wraps in glittering snare
the splintered bones of grass.

Slow moves the hour that sucks our life,
slow drops the late wasp from the pear,
the rose-tree's thread of scent draws thin—
and snaps upon the air.

LAURIE LEE

The Impulse of October

October nights, wild geese string
Yelping garlands along the sky.
Mornings of light frost, grackles stutter
Beadwork jet against the sun.

Life underlines its livingness
Because below the birds, the leaf
Tacks to the inch where it shall lie
All a leaf-forever long.

He moves too, the dull wasp
Cold-diminished, for he wants,
Too, Elysian no-winter.
Stiffly angled, on basement walls

He creeps, in dusty sanctuary,
Grey substitute for the orange South.
In feeble light he is feebly seen.
The careless hand he sickly stings.

W. R. MOSES

Willow Poem

It is a willow when summer is over,
a willow by the river
from which no leaf has fallen nor
bitten by the sun
turned orange or crimson.
The leaves cling and grow paler,
swing and grow paler
over the swirling waters of the river
as if loath to let go,
they are so cool, so drunk with
the swirl of the wind and of the river—
oblivious to winter,
the last to let go and fall
into the water and on the ground.

WILLIAM CARLOS WILLIAMS

Survivor

On an oak in autumn
there'll always be
one leaf left at the top of the tree
that won't let go with the rest and rot—
won't cast loose and skitter and sail
and end in a puddle of rain in a swale
and fatten the earth and be fruitful . . .

                             No,
it won't and it won't and it won't let go.
It rattles a kind of a jig tattoo,
a telegrapher's tattle that *will* get through
like an SOS from a struggling ship
over and over, a dash and a skip.

You cover your head with your quilt and still
that telegrapher's key on Conway hill
calls to Polaris.

                  I can spell:
I know what it says . . . I know too well.
I pull my pillow over my ear
but I hear.

ARCHIBALD MACLEISH

Night Wind in Fall

Air heaves at matter:
The wind makes all the wind noises.
Twig-strain, leaf-scatter,
Tapping of tips on rebuffing windows,
Nut-fall, little shatter
Of rotted small limbs on blunting ground.
Neither metronomic nor constant,
But recurring as metres recur.

I remember "Words alone
Are certain good." I don't hear,
Either in twig-tap, blown-
Leaf sigh, or hissing or whistle
Or scrape, the singular tone
Of a word. Inarticulate wind.
Yet a rising and falling persists.
Words are a rising and falling.

Someone less drowsy
Than I am, might understand,
Might catch, from mousy
Sounds and silences, birdlike
Alternations, from ghostly
Stutters, a viable pattern of words.
Unclogged senses might do it.
There must be senses unclogged

Somewhere. Maybe, I think,
They can decode such words
As bless, from brink to brink,
The whole reach that listens under the wind.
I hope each chink, each link
That forms this house is blessed. And all
Houses. All of the running grass.
Every lake in Canada under the stars.

W. R. MOSES

Winter is Another Country

If the autumn would
End! If the sweet season,
The late light in the tall trees would
End! If the fragrance, the odor of
Fallen apples, dust on the road,
Water somewhere near, the scent of
Water touching me; if this would end
I could endure the absence in the night,
The hands beyond the reach of hands, the name
Called out and never answered with my name:
The image seen but never seen with sight.
I could endure this all
If autumn ended and the cold light came.

ARCHIBALD MACLEISH

Winter

Winter

Now the snow
lies on the ground
and more snow
is descending upon it—
Patches of red dirt
hold together
the old
snow patches

This is winter—
rosettes of
leather-green leaves
by the old fence
and bare trees
marking the sky—

This is winter
winter, winter
leather-green leaves
spearshaped
in the falling snow

WILLIAM CARLOS WILLIAMS

Winter Morning

All night the wind swept over the house
And through our dream,
Swirling the snow up through the pines,
Ruffling the white, ice-capped clapboards,
Rattling the windows,
Rustling around and below our bed
So that we rode
Over wild water
In a white ship breasting the waves.
We rode through the night
On green, marbled
Water, and half-waking, watched
The white, eroded peaks of icebergs
Sail past our windows;
Rode out the night in that north country,
And awoke, the house buried in snow,
Perched on a
Chill promontory, a
Giant's tooth
In the mouth of the cold valley,
Its white tongue looped frozen around us,
The trunks of tall birches
Revealing the rib cage of a whale
Stranded by a still stream;
And saw, through the motionless baleen of their branches,
As if through time,
Light that shone
On a landscape of ivory,
A harbor of bone.

WILLIAM JAY SMITH

Glass World

The still scene scintillates;
sparks swarm over the brier,
bare bushes blaze. Ice
is setting the world on fire.

A touch of sun on the sleet
turns the teasel to crystal,
and glances stars off the glass
stalks of the burdock and thistle.

On enamels of blue, a tree,
kindled by cold, air, and water,
lights up like a chandelier
in a flash of opals and amber.

DOROTHY DONNELLY

Snowy Night

This is like a place
we used to know,
but stranger
and filled with the cold
imagination of a frozen
sea, in which
the moon is anchored
like a ghost
in heavy chains.

JOHN HAINES

A Winter Scene

The noses are running at our house.
Like faucets. Wild horses.
Otherwise it is quiet here;
There is nothing afoot except Lassie who is running
Hastily through a TV pasture in quest of a
TV doctor, while we
Who are not running (except for our noses)
Vegetate (off TV) with Vicks and prescriptions
In an atmosphere so sedentary that if
We ever get well and get up and regain the potential
For running again with more than just our noses,
We may not.
          I mean it is possible
That when we get well we will not undertake to run
Or even to walk (though we'll be able to),
But will hold firm to our sofas and spread our Vicks
Ever more thickly over our throats and chests, letting Lassie
And such other TV characters as may follow
On Channel Five
Do all our running, walking, barking, thinking
For us, once even our noses
Have stopped their incessant running and it is quiet here.

REED WHITTEMORE

Desert Places

Snow falling and night falling fast, oh, fast
In a field I looked into going past,
And the ground almost covered smooth in snow,
But a few weeds and stubble showing last.

The woods around it have it—it is theirs.
All animals are smothered in their lairs.
I am too absent-spirited to count;
The loneliness includes me unawares.

And lonely as it is, that loneliness
Will be more lonely ere it will be less—
A blanker whiteness of benighted snow
With no expression, nothing to express.

They cannot scare me with their empty spaces
Between stars—on stars where no human race is.
I have it in me so much nearer home
To scare myself with my own desert places.

ROBERT FROST

With a Hey, Ho, the Wind and the Rain

Sophistication

When I was a child
I thought that it rained
all over the whole wide world at once,
but now, having grown much wiser,

I know that my neighbor
can receive a deluge,
and my scrap of earth lie here gasping
like a fish tossed onto land,

or that when it pours
it is no monsoon
with the trees before long dripping in sunlight
all in a sweat about nothing.

VASSAR MILLER

King Wind

Of all the weathers wind is king.
Snow would not blow, nor rain beat,
Nor grasses ripple, nor trees break,
Except for the will of this blind thing
That neither is seen nor sees, but anyway
Comes, and anyway goes—from where
To where? Nobody knows.

I never am tired of thinking of him.
Even in sleep—but where is his bed?—
He dreams of filling the world again
With waves of water and walls of air
That neither can stop nor stand, but anyway
Rise, and anyway fall. So on
Forever. Motion is all.

MARK VAN DOREN

Ploughing on Sunday

The white cock's tail
Tosses in the wind.
The turkey-cock's tail
Glitters in the sun.

Water in the fields.
The wind pours down.
The feathers flare
And bluster in the wind.

Remus, blow your horn!
I'm plowing on Sunday,
Ploughing North America.
Blow your horn!

Tum-ti-tum.
Ti-tum-tum-tum!
The turkey-cock's tail
Spreads to the sun.

The white cock's tail
Streams to the moon.
Water in the fields.
The wind pours down.

WALLACE STEVENS

Little Exercise

Think of the storm roaming the sky uneasily
like a dog looking for a place to sleep in,
listen to it growling.

Think how they must look now, the mangrove keys
lying out there unresponsive to the lightning
in dark, coarse-fibred families,

where occasionally a heron may undo his head,
shake up his feathers, make an uncertain comment
when the surrounding water shines.

Think of the boulevard and the little palm trees
all stuck in rows, suddenly revealed
as fistfuls of limp fish-skeletons.

It is raining there. The boulevard
and its broken sidewalks with weeds in every crack,
are relieved to be wet, the sea to be freshened.

Now the storm goes away again in a series
of small, badly lit battle-scenes,
each in "Another part of the field."

Think of someone sleeping in the bottom of a row-boat
tied to a mangrove root or the pile of a bridge;
think of him as uninjured, barely disturbed.

ELIZABETH BISHOP

A Local Storm

The first whimper of the storm
At the back door, wanting in,
Promised no such brave creature
As threatens now to perform
Black rites of the witch Nature
Publicly on our garden.

Thrice he hath circled the house
Murmuring incantations,
Doing a sort of war dance.
Does he think to frighten us
With his so primitive chants
Or merely try our patience?

The danger lies, after all,
In being led to suppose—
With Lear—that the wind dragons
Have been let loose to settle
Some private grudge of heaven's.
Still, how nice for our egos.

DONALD JUSTICE

Squall

In the hazy shape of my mind
I feel the glass fall. My windows
Grow dim.
         When will the weather break,
The doors in me slam to a new wind?
Waiting is one thing and then another,
The track time makes and unmakes.
A song-sparrow calls. The waves
On my shore come like old ocean
Against the stones and sand.
                Gulls
Paddle far out like dirty ducks, loose gatherings
Nose to the wind that hasn't yet come.
But will come before this day dies.
The leaves will all turn wrong side to
And my brain will clatter like
A broken weathercock seeking
Its own north, its own lost
Bearings.

JOHN MOORE

Storm on the Island

We are prepared: we build our houses squat,
Sink walls in rock and roof them with good slate.
This wizened earth has never troubled us
With hay, so, as you see, there are no stacks
Or stooks that can be lost. Nor are there trees
Which might prove company when it blows full
Blast: you know what I mean—leaves and branches
Can raise a tragic chorus in a gale
So that you listen to the thing you fear
Forgetting that it pummels your house too.
But there are no trees, no natural shelter.
You might think that the sea is company,
Exploding comfortably down on the cliffs
But no: when it begins, the flung spray hits
The very windows, spits like a tame cat
Turned savage. We just sit tight while wind dives
And strafes invisibly. Space is a salvo,
We are bombarded by the empty air.
Strange, it is a huge nothing that we fear.

SEAMUS HEANEY

Big Wind

Where were the greenhouses going,
Lunging into the lashing
Wind driving water
So far down the river
All the faucets stopped?—
So we drained the manure-machine
For the steam plant,
Pumping the stale mixture
Into the rusty boilers,
Watching the pressure gauge
Waver over to red,
As the seams hissed
And the live steam
Drove to the far
End of the rose-house,
Where the worst wind was,
Creaking the cypress window-frames,
Cracking so much thin glass
We stayed all night,
Stuffing the holes with burlap;
But she rode it out,
That old rose-house,
She hove into the teeth of it,
The core and pith of that ugly storm,
Ploughing with her stiff prow,
Bucking into the wind-waves
That broke over the whole of her,
Flailing her sides with spray,
Flinging long strings of wet across the roof-top,
Finally veering, wearing themselves out, merely
Whistling thinly under the wind-vents;
She sailed until the calm morning,
Carrying her full cargo of roses.

THEODORE ROETHKE

Hurricane

Sleep at noon. Window blind
rattle and bang. Pay no mind.
Door go jump like somebody coming:
let him come. Tin roof drumming:
drum away—she's drummed before.
Blinds blow loose: unlatch the door.
Look up sky through the manchineel:
black show through like a hole in your heel.
Look down shore at the old canoe:
rag-a-tag sea turn white, turn blue,
lick up dust in the lee of the reef,
wallop around like a loblolly leaf.
Let her wallop—who's afraid?
Gale from the north-east: just the Trade . . .

And that's when you hear it: far and high—
sea-birds screaming down the sky
high and far like screaming leaves;
tree-branch slams across the eaves;
rain like pebbles on the ground . . .

and the sea turns white and the wind goes round.

ARCHIBALD MACLEISH

Brainstorm

The house was shaken by a rising wind
That rattled window and door. He sat alone
In an upstairs room and heard these things: a blind
Ran up with a bang, a door slammed, a groan
Came from some hidden joist, and a leaky tap,
At any silence of the wind, walked like
A blind man through the house. Timber and sap
Revolt, he thought, from washer, baulk and spike.
Bent to his book, continued unafraid
Until the crows came down from their loud flight
To walk along the rooftree overhead.
Their horny feet, so near but out of sight,
Scratched on the slate; when they were blown away
He heard their wings beat till they came again,
While the wind rose, and the house seemed to sway,
And window panes began to blind with rain.
The house was talking, not to him, he thought,
But to the crows; the crows were talking back
In their black voices. The secret might be out:
Houses are only trees stretched on the rack.
And once the crows knew, all nature would know.
Fur, leaf and feather would invade the form,
Nail rust with rain and shingle warp with snow,
Vine tear the wall, till any straw-borne storm
Could rip both roof and rooftree off and show
Naked to nature what they had kept warm.

He came to feel the crows walk on his head
As if he were the house, their crooked feet
Scratched, through the hair, his scalp. He might be dead,
It seemed, and all the noises underneath
Be but the cooling of the sinews, veins,
Juices, and sodden sacks suddenly let go;
While in his ruins of wiring, his burst mains,
The rainy wind had been set free to blow

Until the green uprising and mob rule
That ran the world had taken over him,
Split him like seed, and set him in the school
Where any crutch can learn to be a limb.

Inside his head he heard the stormy crows.

HOWARD NEMEROV

The Storm

FORIO D'ISCHIA

I

Against the stone breakwater,
Only an ominous lapping,
While the wind whines overhead,
Coming down from the mountain,
Whistling between the arbors, the winding terraces;
A thin whine of wires, a rattling and flapping of leaves,
And the small street-lamp swinging and slamming against the lamp-pole.

Where have the people gone?
There is one light on the mountain.

II

Along the sea-wall, a steady sloshing of the swell,
The waves not yet high, but even,
Coming closer and closer upon each other;
A fine fume of rain driving in from the sea,
Riddling the sand, like a wide spray of buckshot,
The wind from the sea and the wind from the mountain contending,
Flicking the foam from the whitecaps straight upward into the darkness.

A time to go home!—
And a child's dirty shift billows upward out of an alley,
A cat runs from the wind as we do,
Between the whitening trees, up Santa Lucia,
Where the heavy door unlocks,
And our breath comes more easy,—
Then a crack of thunder, and the black rain runs over us, over
The flat-roofed houses, coming down in gusts, beating
The walls, the slatted windows, driving
The last watcher indoors, moving the cardplayers closer
To their cards, their anisette.

III

We creep to our bed, and its straw mattress.
We wait; we listen.
The storm lulls off, then redoubles,
Bending the trees half-way down to the ground,
Shaking loose the last wizened oranges in the orchard,
Flattening the limber carnations.

A spider eases himself down from a swaying light-bulb,
Running over the coverlet, down under the iron bedstead.
The bulb goes on and off, weakly.
Water roars in the cistern.

We lie closer on the gritty pillow,
Breathing heavily, hoping—
For the great last leap of the wave over the breakwater,
The flat boom on the beach of the towering sea-swell,
The sudden shudder as the jutting sea-cliff collapses,
And the hurricane drives the dead straw into the living pine-tree.

THEODORE ROETHKE

Rain in the Desert

The huge red-buttressed mesa over yonder
Is merely a far-off temple where the sleepy sun is burning
Its altar fires of pinyon and toyon for the day.

The old priests sleep, white-shrouded;
Their pottery whistles lie beside them, the prayer-sticks closely feathered.

On every mummied face there glows a smile.

The sun is rolling slowly
Beneath the sluggish folds of the sky-serpents,
Coiling, uncoiling, blue-black, sparked with fires.

The old dead priests
Feel in the thin dried earth that is heaped about them,
Above the smell of scorching, oozing pinyon,
The acrid smell of rain.

And now the showers
Surround the mesa like a troop of silver dancers:
Shaking their rattles, stamping, chanting, roaring,
Whirling, extinguishing the last red wisp of light.

JOHN GOULD FLETCHER

Atavism

Rain,
Million-footed requiem of the rain:
Rain in our hearts, and we feed upon
Gloom, and there are gray plains there,
Bitter with sagebrush, and the coulees choked
With yellow water, and the mountains far.

We are in the mountains, riding the summit,
Fog blows out of the canyons, spruces drip;
They are depressed, their shoulders slump, they gloom
Forebodingly. Our saddles are wet but we love
The rain still, the black spruces, the fog blowing.
(Even the ugly cities share in the rain
with beautiful things.)
                              We come to the trail going down,
And pull up, and sit, and water drips from our boots;
We can see the fog thinning in the balsams below;
There will be hot grub and a dry bed and a long
Drowse by the fire, with our minds full of the rain
And the deep night, and sleep, and the pines dripping.

RICHARD LAKE

After Rain

The rain of a night and a day and a night
Stops at the light
Of this pale choked day. The peering sun
Sees what has been done.
The road under the trees has a border new
Of purple hue
Inside the border of bright thin grass:
For all that has
Been left by November of leaves is torn
From hazel and thorn
And the greater trees. Throughout the copse
No dead leaf drops
On grey grass, green moss, burnt-orange fern,
At the wind's return;
The leaflets out of the ash-tree shed
Are thinly spread
In the road, like little black fish, inlaid,
As if they played.
What hangs from the myriad branches down there
So hard and bare
Is twelve yellow apples lovely to see
On one crab tree.
And on each twig of every tree in the dell
Uncountable
Crystals both dark and bright of the rain
That begins again.

EDWARD THOMAS

Father

of

the

Man

You're

Clownlike, happiest on your hands,
Feet to the stars, and moon-skulled,
Gilled like a fish. A common-sense
Thumbs-down on the dodo's mode.
Wrapped up in yourself like a spool,
Trawling your dark as owls do.
Mute as a turnip from the Fourth
Of July to All Fool's Day.
O high-riser, my little loaf.

Vague as fog and looked for like mail.
Farther off than Australia.
Bent-backed Atlas, our travelled prawn.
Snug as a bud and at home
Like a sprat in a pickle jug.
A creel of eels, all ripples.
Jumpy as a Mexican bean.
Right, like a well-done sum.
A clean slate, with your own face on.

SYLVIA PLATH

Chinese Baby Asleep

She has the immaculate look of the new,
like the bud of the rose just showing through
its shell of separating sepals.

That seal with the sheen of silk, her skin,
encircles a seedling sun within
as rinds go round the stars in apples.

Eyelid and lip are luminous, lit
by the glow of life, by her breath as it
flows in and out like light through opals.

DOROTHY DONNELLY

Balloons

Since Christmas they have lived with us,
Guileless and clear,
Oval soul-animals,
Taking up half the space,
Moving and rubbing on the silk

Invisible air drifts,
Giving a shriek and pop
When attacked, then scooting to rest, barely trembling,
Yellow cathead, blue fish—
Such queer moons we live with

Instead of dead furniture!
Straw mats, white walls
And these travelling
Globes of thin air, red, green,
Delighting

The heart like wishes or free
Peacocks blessing
Old ground with a feather
Beaten in starry metals.
Your small

Brother is making
His balloon squeak like a cat.
Seeming to see
A funny pink world he might eat on the other side of it,
He bites
Then sits
Back, fat jug
Contemplating a world clear as water,
A red
Shred in his little fist.

SYLVIA PLATH

The Child

He lives among a dog,
a tricycle, and a friend.
Nobody owns him.

He walks by himself, beside
the black pool, in the cave
where icicles of rock

rain hard water,
and the walls are rough
with the light of stone.

He hears low talking
without words.
The hand of a wind touches him.

He walks until he is tired
or somebody calls him.
He leaves right away.

When he plays with his friend
he stops suddenly
to hear the black water.

DONALD HALL

Janet Waking

Beautifully Janet slept
Till it was deeply morning. She woke then
And thought about her dainty-feathered hen,
To see how it had kept.

One kiss she gave her mother.
Only a small one gave she to her daddy
Who would have kissed each curl of his shining baby;
No kiss at all for her brother.

"Old Chucky, old Chucky!" she cried,
Running across the world upon the grass
To Chucky's house, and listening. But alas,
Her Chucky had died.

It was a transmogrifying bee
Came droning down on Chucky's old bald head
And sat and put the poison. It scarcely bled,
But how exceedingly

And purply did the knot
Swell with the venom and communicate
Its rigor! Now the poor comb stood up straight
But Chucky did not.

So there was Janet
Kneeling on the wet grass, crying her brown hen
(Translated far beyond the daughters of men)
To rise and walk upon it.

And weeping fast as she had breath
Janet implored us, "Wake her from her sleep!"
And would not be instructed in how deep
Was the forgetful kingdom of death.

JOHN CROWE RANSOM

From "Heart's Needle"

Here in the scuffled dust
  is our ground of play.
I lift you on your swing and must
  shove you away,
see you return again,
  drive you off again, then

stand quiet till you come.
  You, though you climb
higher, farther from me, longer,
  will fall back to me stronger.
Bad penny, pendulum,
  you keep my constant time

to bob in blue July
  where fat goldfinches fly
over the glittering, fecund
  reach of our growing lands.
Once more now, this second,
  I hold you in my hands.

W. D. SNODGRASS

The Party

They served tea in the sandpile, together with
Mudpies baked on the sidewalk.
After tea
The youngest said that he had had a good dinner,
The oldest dressed for a dance,
And they sallied forth together with watering pots
To moisten a rusted fire truck on account of it
Might rain.

I watched from my study,
Thought of my part in these contributions to world
Gaiety, and resolved
That the very least acknowledgment I could make
Would be to join them;
              so we
All took our watering pots (filled with pies)
And poured tea on our dog. Then I kissed the children
And told them that when they grew up we would have
Real tea parties.
"That did be fun!" the youngest shouted, and ate pies
With wild surmise.

REED WHITTEMORE

Early Supper

Laughter of children brings
    The kitchen down with laughter.
While the old kettle sings
Laughter of children brings
To a boil all savory things.
    Higher than beam or rafter,
Laughter of children brings
    The kitchen down with laughter.

So ends an autumn day,
    Light ripples on the ceiling,
Dishes are stacked away;
So ends an autumn day,
The children jog and sway
    In comic dances wheeling.
So ends an autumn day,
    Light ripples on the ceiling.

They trail upstairs to bed,
    And night is a dark tower.
The kettle calls: instead
They trail upstairs to bed,
Leaving warmth, the coppery-red
    Mood of their carnival hour.
They trail upstairs to bed,
    And night is a dark tower.

BARBARA HOWES

Daedalus

My son has birds in his head.

I know them now. I catch
the pitch of their calls, their shrill
cacophanies, their chitterings, their coos.
They hover behind his eyes, and come to rest
on a branch, on a book, grow still,
claws curled, wings furled.
His is a bird world.

I learn the flutter of his moods,
his moments of swoop and soar.
From the ground, I feel him try
the limits of the air—
sudden lift, sudden terror—
and move in time to cradle
his quivering, feathered fear.

At evening, in the tower,
I see him to sleep, and see
the hooding over of eyes,
the slow folding of wings.
I wake to his morning twitterings,
to the *croomb* of his becoming.

He chooses his selves—wren, hawk,
swallow, or owl—to explore
the trees and rooftops of his heady wishing.
Tomtit, birdwit.
Am I to call him down, to give him
a grounding, teach him gravity?

Gently, gently.
Time tells us what we weigh, and soon enough
his feet will reach the ground.
Age, like a cage, will enclose him.
So the wise men said.

My son has birds in his head.

ALASTAIR REID

Mousemeal

My son invites me to witness with him
a children's program, a series of cartoons,
on television. Addressing myself to share
his harmless pleasures, I am horrified
by the unbridled violence and hostility
of the imagined world he takes in stride,
where human beings dressed in the skins of mice
are eaten by portcullises and cowcatchers,
digested through the winding corridors
of organs, overshoes, boa constrictors
and locomotive boilers, to be excreted
in waters where shark and squid and abalone
wait to employ their tentacles and jaws.
It seems there is no object in this world
unable to become a gullet with great lonely teeth;
sometimes a set of teeth all by itself
comes clacking over an endless plain
after the moving mouse; and though the mouse
wins in the end, the tail of one cartoon
is spliced into the mouth of the next, where his
rapid and trivial agony repeats itself
in another form. My son has seen these things
a number of times, and knows what to expect;
he does not seem disturbed or anything more
than mildly amused. Maybe these old cartoons
refer to my childhood and not to his
(The ogres in them wear Mussolini's face),
so that when mice are swallowed by skeletons
or empty suits of armor, when a tribe
of savage Negro mice is put through a wringer
and stacked flat in the cellar, he can take
the objective and critical view, while I
am shaken to see the giant picassoid
parents eating and voiding their little mice
time and again. And when the cheery announcer
cries, "Well, kids, that's the end," my son gets up
obediently and runs outside to play.
I hope he will ride over this world as well,
and that his crudest and most terrifying dreams
will not return with such wide publicity.

HOWARD NEMEROV

Child on Top of a Greenhouse

The wind billowing out the seat of my britches,
My feet crackling splinters of glass and dried putty,
The half-grown chrysanthemums staring up like accusers,
Up through the streaked glass, flashing with sunlight,
A few white clouds all rushing eastward,
A line of elms plunging and tossing like horses,
And everyone, everyone pointing up and shouting!

THEODORE ROETHKE

Eleven

And summer mornings the mute child, rebellious,
Stupid, hating the words, the meanings, hating
The Think now, Think, the Oh but Think! would leave
On tiptoe the three chairs on the verandah
And crossing tree by tree the empty lawn
Push back the shed door and upon the sill
Stand pressing out the sunlight from his eyes
And enter and with outstretched fingers feel
The grindstone and behind it the bare wall
And turn and in the corner on the cool
Hard earth sit listening. And one by one,
Out of the dazzled shadow in the room,
The shapes would gather, the brown plowshare, spades,
Mattocks, the polished helves of picks, a scythe
Hung from the rafters, shovels, slender tines
Glinting across the curve of sickles—shapes
Older than men were, the wise tools, the iron
Friendly with earth. And sit there, quiet, breathing
The harsh dry smell of withered bulbs, the faint
Odor of dung, the silence. And outside
Beyond the half-shut door the blind leaves
And the corn moving. And at noon would come,
Up from the garden, his hard crooked hands
Gentle with earth, his knees still earth-stained, smelling
Of sun, of summer, the old gardener, like
A priest, like an interpreter, and bend
Over his baskets.   And they would not speak:
They would say nothing. And the child would sit there
Happy as though he had no name, as though
He had been no one: like a leaf, a stem,
Like a root growing—

ARCHIBALD MACLEISH

Farm Boy After Summer

A seated statue of himself he seems.
A bronze slowness becomes him. Patently
The page he contemplates he doesn't see.

The lesson, the long lesson, has been summer.
His mind holds summer as his skin holds sun.
For once the homework, all of it, was done.

What were the crops, where were the fiery fields
Where for so many days so many hours
The sun assaulted him with glittering showers?

Expect a certain absence in his presence.
Expect all winter long a summer scholar,
For scarcely all its snows can cool that color.

ROBERT FRANCIS

When
I Was
a
Child

Invocation

Unwinding the spool of the morning,
the cicada spins his green song,
dream deeper than sleep's,

drawing me back through the lost years,
fumbling an invisible knob
on a hidden door,

a door I have always known waited
if I could but touch it to substance
and out of enchantment.

Cicada, cicada, fey doorman,
loop my heart in your skein till
my foot finds your lintel.

VASSAR MILLER

Memory of a Porch

MIAMI, 1942

What I remember
Is how the wind chime
Commenced to stir
As she spoke of her childhood,

As though the simple
Death of a pet cat,
Buried with flowers,

Had brought to the porch
Some rumor of storms
Dying out over
A dark Atlantic.

At least I heard
The thing begin—
A thin, skeletal music—

And in the deep silence
Below all memory
The sighing of ferns
Half-asleep in their boxes.

DONALD JUSTICE

Bears

Wonderful bears that walked my room all night,
Where are you gone, your sleek and fairy fur,
Your eyes' veiled imperious light?

Brown bears as rich as mocha or as musk,
White opalescent bears whose fur stood out
Electric in the deepening dusk,

And great black bears who seemed more blue than black,
More violet than blue against the dark—
Where are you now? upon what track

Mutter your muffled paws, that used to tread
So softly, surely, up the creakless stair
While I lay listening in bed?

When did I lose you? whose have you become?
Why do I wait and wait and never hear
Your thick nocturnal pacing in my room?
My bears, who keeps you now, in pride and fear?

ADRIENNE RICH

The Sleeping Giant

A HILL, SO NAMED, IN HAMDEN, CONNECTICUT

The whole day long, under the walking sun
That poised an eye on me from its high floor,
Holding my toy beside the clapboard house
I looked for him, the summer I was four.

I was afraid the waking arm would break
From the loose earth and rub against his eyes
A fist of trees, and the whole country tremble
In the exultant labor of his rise;

Then he with giant steps in the small streets
Would stagger, cutting off the sky, to seize
The roofs from house and home because we had
Covered his shape with dirt and planted trees;

And then kneel down and rip with fingernails
A trench to pour the enemy Atlantic
Into our basin, and the water rush,
With the streets full and all the voices frantic.

That was the summer I expected him.
Later the high and watchful sun instead
Walked low behind the house, and school began,
And winter pulled a sheet over his head.

DONALD HALL

Mouse Night: One of Our Games

We heard thunder. Nothing great—on high
ground rain began. Who ran through
that rain? I shrank, a fieldmouse, when
the thunder came—under grass with bombs
of water scything stems. My tremendous
father cowered: "Lions rushing make
that sound," he said; "we'll be brain-washed
for sure if head-size chunks of water hit us.
Duck and cover! It takes a man
to be a mouse this night," he said.

WILLIAM STAFFORD

Manners

FOR A CHILD OF 1918

My grandfather said to me
as we sat on the wagon seat,
"Be sure to remember to always
speak to everyone you meet."

We met a stranger on foot.
My grandfather's whip tapped his hat.
"Good day, sir. Good day. A fine day."
And I said it and bowed where I sat.

Then we overtook a boy we knew
with his big pet crow on his shoulder.
"Always offer everyone a ride;
don't forget that when you get older,"

my grandfather said. So Willy
climbed up with us, but the crow
gave a "Caw!" and flew off. I was worried.
How would he know where to go?

But he flew a little way at a time
from fence post to fence post, ahead;
and when Willy whistled he answered.
"A fine bird," my grandfather said,

"and he's well brought up. See, he answers
nicely when he's spoken to.
Man or beast, that's good manners.
Be sure that you both always do."

When automobiles went by,
the dust hid the people's faces,
but we shouted "Good day! Good day!
Fine day!" at the top of our voices.

When we came to Hustler Hill,
he said that the mare was tired,
so we all got down and walked,
as our good manners required.

ELIZABETH BISHOP

Digging for China

"Far enough down is China," somebody said.
"Dig deep enough and you might see the sky
As clear as at the bottom of a well.
Except it would be a real—a different sky.
Then you could burrow down until you came
To China! Oh, it's nothing like New Jersey.
There's people, trees, and houses, and all that,
But much, much different. Nothing looks the same."

I went and got the trowel out of the shed
And sweated like a coolie all that morning,
Digging a hole beside the lilac-bush,
Down on my hands and knees. It was a sort
Of praying, I suspect. I watched my hand
Dig deep and darker, and I tried and tried
To dream a place where nothing was the same.
The trowel never did break through to blue.

Before the dream could weary of itself
My eyes were tired of looking into darkness,
My sunbaked head of hanging down a hole.
I stood up in a place I had forgotten,
Blinking and staggering while the earth went round
And showed me silver barns, the fields dozing
In palls of brightness, patens growing and gone
In the tides of leaves, and the whole sky china blue.
Until I got my balance back again
All that I saw was China, China, China.

RICHARD WILBUR

The Remorse for Time

When I was a boy, I used to go to bed
By daylight, in the summer, and lie awake
Between the cool, white, reconciling sheets,
Hearing the talk of birds, watching the light
Diminish through the shimmering planes of leaf
Outside the window, until sleep came down
When darkness did, eyes closing as the light
Faded out of them, silencing the birds.

Sometimes still, in the sleepless dark hours
Tormented most by the remorse for time,
Only for time, the mind speaks of that boy
(he did no wrong, then why had he to die?)
Falling asleep on the current of the stars
Which even then washed him away past pardon.

HOWARD NEMEROV

First Confession

Blood thudded in my ears. I scuffed,
   Steps stubborn, to the telltale booth
Beyond whose curtained portal coughed
   The robed repositor of truth.

The slat shot back. The universe
   Bowed down his cratered dome to hear
Enumerated my each curse,
   The sip snitched from my old man's beer,

My sloth pride envy lechery,
   The dime held back from Peter's Pence
With which I'd bribed my girl to pee
   That I might spy her instruments.

Hovering scale-pans when I'd done
   Settled their balance slow as silt
While in the restless dark I burned
   Bright as a brimstone in my guilt

Until as one feeds birds he doled
   Seven Our Fathers and a Hail
Which I to double-scrub my soul
   Intoned twice at the altar rail

Where Sunday in seraphic light
   I knelt, as full of grace as most,
And stuck my tongue out at the priest:
   A fresh roost for the Holy Ghost.

X. J. KENNEDY

I, Icarus

There was a time when I could fly. I swear it.
Perhaps, if I think hard for a moment, I can even tell you the year.
My room was on the ground floor at the rear of the house.
My bed faced a window.
Night after night I lay on my bed and willed myself to fly.
It was hard work, I can tell you.
Sometimes I lay perfectly still for an hour before I felt my body
        rising from the bed.
I rose slowly, slowly, until I floated three or four feet above
        the floor.
Then, with a kind of swimming motion, I propelled myself toward
        the window.

Outside, I rose higher and higher, above the pasture fence,
        above the clothesline, above the dark, haunted trees
        beyond the pasture.
And, all the time, I heard the music of the flutes.
It seemed the wind made this music.
And sometimes there were voices singing.
All of this was a long time ago and I cannot remember the words
        the voices sang,
But I know I flew when I heard them.

ALDEN NOWLAN

Running

What were we playing? Was it prisoner's base?
I ran with whacking keds
Down the cart-road past Rickard's place,
And where it dropped beside the tractor-sheds

Leapt out into the air above a blurred
Terrain, through jolted light,
Took two hard lopes, and at the third
Spanked off a hummock-side exactly right,

And made the turn, and with delighted strain
Sprinted across the flat
By the bull-pen, and up the lane.
Thinking of happiness, I think of that.

RICHARD WILBUR

Robin Hood

Robin Hood
When I was twelve,
In your greenwood
How I would selve
Myself, rob rich
Legend to give
Poor everyday.
With you I'd rive
The willow-switch
And our sword-play
Left Gisbourne in
A bestial skin.
And with you, hale
At the Blue Boar Inn,
I drank brown ale,
Clanked nipperkin
With Allan-a-Dale,
Took Stutely from
His gallows cart,
Saw Sheriff pale
And King smart
When finger and thumb,
Unmatched, would loose
Clothyard shaft
And the grey goose
Feather flew
And arrow sang
A song more true
Than art or craft
Or history knew.

GRAY BURR

Young

A thousand doors ago
when I was a lonely kid
in a big house with four
garages and it was summer
as long as I could remember,
I lay on the lawn at night,
clover wrinkling under me,
the wise stars bedding over me,
my mother's window a funnel
of yellow heat running out,
my father's window, half shut,
an eye where sleepers pass,
and the boards of the house
were smooth and white as wax
and probably a million leaves
sailed on their strange stalks
as the crickets ticked together
and I, in my brand new body,
which was not a woman's yet,
told the stars my questions
and thought God could really see
the heat and the painted light,
elbows, knees, dreams, goodnight.

ANNE SEXTON

The Whipping

The old woman across the way
    is whipping the boy again
and shouting to the neighborhood
    her goodness and his wrongs.

Wildly he crashes through elephant ears,
    pleads in dusty zinnias,
while she in spite of crippling fat
    pursues and corners him.

She strikes and strikes the shrilly circling
    boy till the stick breaks
in her hand. His tears are rainy weather
    to woundlike memories.

My head gripped in bony vise
    of knees, the writhing struggle
to wrench free, the blows, the fear
    worse than blows that hateful

Words could bring, the face that I
    no longer knew or loved . . .
Well, it is over now, it is over,
    and the boy sobs in his room,

And the woman leans muttering against
    a tree, exhausted, purged—
avenged in part for lifelong hidings
    she has had to bear.

ROBERT HAYDEN

The Tree Is Father to the Man

By all the laws
we should have been cracked into splinters;
broken down
into hard-working people
heads stuck
in the checkbook.

By all the laws
we should have been dead
               (where it counts)

far down
where things grow.

O, all the laws!
But the tree showed us
              possibilities!

Black tree
bombarded by incinerators
standing in shadow
on a 2 × 2 plot.
Once a year
not only leaves! but fruit!
small green
apples, perfect for window cracking.

LOU LIPSITZ

A
Beautiful
Brief
Moment

Nothing Gold Can Stay

Nature's first green is gold,
Her hardest hue to hold,
Her early leaf's a flower:
But only so an hour,
Then leaf subsides to leaf.
So Eden sank to grief,
So dawn goes down to day.
Nothing gold can stay.

ROBERT FROST

Watering the Horse

How strange to think of giving up all ambition!
Suddenly I see with such clear eyes
The white flake of snow
That has just fallen on the horse's mane!

ROBERT BLY

The Snowflake

Before I melt,
Come, look at me!
This lovely icy filigree!
Of a great forest
In one night
I make a wilderness
Of white:
By skyey cold
Of crystals made,
All softly, on
Your finger laid,
I pause, that you
My beauty see:
Breathe, and I vanish
Instantly.

WALTER DE LA MARE

The Harbor

Passing through huddled and ugly walls,
By doorways where women
Looked from their hunger-deep eyes,
Haunted with shadows of hunger-hands,
Out from the huddled and ugly walls,
I came sudden, at the city's edge,
On a blue burst of lake—
Long lake waves breaking under the sun
On a spray-flung curve of shore;
And a fluttering storm of gulls,
Masses of great gray wings
And flying white bellies
Veering and wheeling free in the open.

CARL SANDBURG

Recollection

Softly the crane's foot crumples a star
    That lies upon the lake;
Bird stalking frog leaves light
    Littered in its wake.

The scattered star collects itself
    Upon the water's fold;
Heel cannot bruise, nor weight break
    The shadow shape of gold.

DOROTHY DONNELLY

Egrets

Once as I travelled through a quiet evening,
I saw a pool, jet-black and mirror still.
Beyond, the slender paperbarks stood crowding;
each on its own white image looked its fill,
and nothing moved but thirty egrets wading—
thirty egrets in a quiet evening.

Once in a lifetime, lovely past believing,
your lucky eyes may light on such a pool.
As though for many years I had been waiting,
I watched in silence, till my heart was full
of clear dark water, and white trees unmoving,
and, whiter yet, those egrets wading.

JUDITH WRIGHT

Questioning Faces

The winter owl banked just in time to pass
And save herself from breaking window glass.
And her wings straining suddenly aspread
Caught color from the last of evening red
In a display of underdown and quill
To glassed-in children at the window sill.

ROBERT FROST

The Child at Winter Sunset

The child at winter sunset,
Holding her breath in adoration of the peacock's tail
That spread its red—ah, higher and higher—
Wept suddenly. "It's going!"

The great fan folded;
Shortened; and at last no longer fought the cold, the dark.
And she on the lawn, comfortless by her father,
Shivered, shivered. "It's gone!"

"Yes, this time. But wait,
Darling. There will be other nights—some of them even better."
"Oh, no. It died." He laughed. But she did not.
It was her first glory.

Laid away now in its terrible
Lead coffin, it was the first brightness she had ever
Mourned. "Oh, no, it's dead." And he her father
Mourned too, for more to come.

MARK VAN DOREN

Boy in the Roman Zoo

TO THE FLAMINGOS

                    Ravished arms,
delighted eyes—and all the rest,
parental cautions and alarms,
treacherous sidewalks and his best
blue suit forgotten. He has seen
heaven upon the further shore
and nothing in the null between
has mere existence anymore.
Those shapes of rose, those coals of ice,
command him as love never has
and only they can now suffice.
Forgotten is the child he was,
unguessed the man he will be. One
moment, free of both, he'll run
toward the flamingos in the sun.

ARCHIBALD MACLEISH

A
Kiss
for
Eve

Falling in Love

The heart, that hideous bear,
Sluggish and winter-gaunt,
Shuffles from his leafy lair.
His alarm clock has gone off.
Rumpled, with a cranky cough,
He's out on an early morning jaunt,
And it will take him the Lord knows where.
He's after the prize of the honey tree
That stood in his long winter dream,
And the bushes, heavily bearing there,
So unmistakably blueberry,
And fat trout in the flashing stream.
The branches are thick with birds that sing
The sweet messages of the air,
And the heart's awakening.

DAVID PERKINS

Eden

FOUND POEM FROM THE LIPS
OF SEAN THOMAS, AGED 4

When I kiss Eve
all the clothes dance
and all the boys jump up on to the roof
                                    And
do you know what the dinner does?
The dinner comes down from the big school
then it lays itself on the tables
and eats itself up
Do you know what the plates do?
They gather themselves up
they go to Mrs. Herd
they get into the washing-basin
they wash themselves
and they put themselves back on the shelves
                                    And
do you know what the pictures do?
They come down
throw the old ones in the fire
then the crayons get out
pull out a piece of paper
they draw another picture
then the sellotape comes out of the cupboard
and sticks the pictures up
                                    And
do you know what the school does?
The school pulls itself down
and builds itself up into a church

When I kiss Eve
magic-stuff comes
out through our mouths and

Do you know what the plants do?
They all die
then the seeds in the bag

come into the garden
then they pop into the ground
                              And
do you know what the trees do?
They spring themselves down and die
the seeds walk about
in the mud
and the wind comes along and blows over them
and grows up into appletrees and
cherrytrees grow up
then some sunflowers came
and tulips came
and roses came
                         And and
do you know what the lights do?
They come down
the bulbs go to the shop
to buy another bulb
Do you know what the piano does?
The piano plays itself and
all the toys jump
and play with themselves
                              And
do you know what the sky does?
All the sky jumps down
in the night it did
the sun fell the wind dropped
and half the world fell down and
all the flies were dead
and all the wasps were dead
no more flies and no more wasps
                              And
                              And
                              And
do you know what the plates do?
They gather themselves up . . .

D. M. THOMAS

Only for Me

When I was twelve in that far land,
And was in love with summer nights,
And was in love with Linda Jane,
Whose very name was dancing lights
About my dark, my country bed,
Once I dreamed that she was dead.

And woke; and not one window star,
As I looked out, but wept for me.
I looked again, and my own tears,
Like magic lanterns, made me see
The very eyes of Linda Jane
Weeping everywhere like rain.

Then the sunrise, cool and red,
And then the new day, white and hot.
And after that the growing up
And the forgetting—oh, but not
The selfless woe of one that died.
Only for me, for me she cried.

MARK VAN DOREN

Love

if not necessary, is essential,
is to its season as a Ferris wheel
to its fair.
One moment we are standing
whole on the sidewalk, paying,
joking—there
is nothing to it—and then, bang, a bar
cuts off our legs, and we are
hooked out and rocked back and forth,
airsick even before earth pushes us off.

MOV-
ing into orbit is awful. We ride
grimly, hanging on to ourselves inside.
One insect
and three rust spots on the bones
of the box which holds our bones
are what protect
us, until, thank God, we are able to look down
where everything is changing size
but not shape, as the roofs rise
and subside delightfully, and the ground

BREATHES,
and we breathe too, for the first time. We love
being perpendicular and aloof
while the rest
of the world rolls over and
over and over on the land.
But the best
of it is, we can say just what we please.
"Look out!" we shout to the pigmies
beneath us. "You are going to go
down," and they don't understand, and they do.

OF
the end we remember exactly how
helpless we felt, pausing in the air two
or three times,

falling in stages. When we
get off we are so dizzy
we sometimes
wonder if earth can be depended upon.
Later we get used to it.
Flatness, we have to admit,
is fact. And tomorrow the fair will be gone.

ANNE STEVENSON

The Picnic

It is the picnic with Ruth in the spring.
Ruth was third on my list of seven girls
But the first two were gone (Betty) or else
Had someone (Ellen has accepted Doug).
Indian Gully the last day of school;
Girls make the lunches for the boys too.
I wrote a note to Ruth in algebra class
Day before the test. She smiled, and nodded.
We left the cars and walked through the young corn
The shoots green as paint and the leaves like tongues
Trembling. Beyond the fence where we stood
Some wild strawberry flowered by an elm tree
And Jack-in-the-pulpit was olive ripe.
A blackbird fled as I crossed, and showed
A spot of gold or red under its quick wing.
I held the wire for Ruth and watched the whip
Of her long, striped skirt as she followed.
Three freckles blossomed on her thin, white back
Underneath the loop where the blouse buttoned.
We went for our lunch away from the rest,
Stretched in the new grass, our heads close
Over unknown things wrapped up in wax papers.
Ruth tried for the same, I forget what it was,
And our hands were together. She laughed,
And a breeze caught the edge of her little
Collar and the edge of her brown, loose hair
That touched my cheek. I turned my face in-
to the gentle fall. I saw how sweet it smelled.
She didn't move her head or take her hand.
I felt a soft caving in my stomach
As at the top of the highest slide
When I had been a child, but was not afraid,
And did not know why my eyes moved with wet
As I brushed her cheek with my lips and brushed
Her lips with my own lips. She said to me
Jack, Jack, different than I had ever heard,
Because she wasn't calling me, I think,
Or telling me. She used my name to
Talk in another way I wanted to know.

She laughed again and then she took her hand;
I gave her what we both had touched—can't
Remember what it was, and we ate lunch.
Afterward we walked in the small, cool creek
Our shoes off, her skirt hitched, and she smiling,
My pants rolled, and then we climbed up the high
Side of Indian Gully and looked
Where we had been, our hands together again.
It was then some bright thing came in my eyes,
Starting at the back of them and flowing
Suddenly through my head and down my arms
And stomach and my bare legs that seemed not
To stop in feet, not to feel the red earth
Of the Gully, as though we hung in a
Touch of birds. There was a word in my throat
With the feeling and I knew the first time
What it meant and I said, it's beautiful.
Yes, she said, and I felt the sound and word
In my hand join the sound and word in hers
As in one name said, or in one cupped hand.
We put back on our shoes and socks and we
Sat in the grass awhile, crosslegged, under
A blowing tree, not saying anything.
And Ruth played with shells she found in the creek,
As I watched. Her small wrist which was so sweet
To me turned by her breast and the shells dropped
Green, white, blue, easily into her lap,
Passing light through themselves. She gave the pale
Shells to me, and got up and touched her hips
With her light hands, and we walked down slowly
To play the school games with the others.

JOHN LOGAN

Blackberry Sweet

Black girl black girl
lips as curved as cherries
full as grape bunches
sweet as blackberries

Black girl black girl
when you walk you are
magic as a rising bird
or a falling star

Black girl black girl
what's your spell to make
the heart in my breast
jump   stop   shake

DUDLEY RANDALL

"sweet spring is your
time is my time is our
time for springtime is lovetime
and viva sweet love"

(all the merry little birds are
flying in the floating in the
very spirits singing in
are winging in the blossoming)

lovers go and lovers come
awandering awondering
but any two are perfectly
alone there's nobody else alive

(such a sky and such a sun
i never knew and neither did you
and everybody never breathed
quite so many kinds of yes)

not a tree can count his leaves
each herself by opening
but shining who by thousands mean
only one amazing thing

(secretly adoring shyly
tiny winging darting floating
merry in the blossoming
always joyful selves are singing)

"sweet spring is your
time is my time is our
time for springtime is lovetime
and viva sweet love"

E. E. CUMMINGS

Love Song

I was
the girl of the chain letter,
the girl full of talk of coffins and keyholes,
the one of the telephone bills,
the wrinkled photo and the lost connections,
the one who kept saying—
Listen! Listen!
We must never! We must never!
and all those things . . .

the one
with her eyes half under her coat,
with her large gun-metal blue eyes,
with the thin vein at the bend of her neck
that hummed like a tuning fork,
with her shoulders as bare as a building,
with her thin foot and her thin toes,
with an old red hook in her mouth,
the mouth that kept bleeding
into the terrible fields of her soul . . .

the one who kept dropping off to sleep,
as old as a stone she was,
each hand like a piece of cement,
for hours and hours
and then she'd wake,
after the small death,
and then she'd be as soft as,
as delicate as . . .

as soft and delicate as
an excess of light,
with nothing dangerous at all,
like a beggar who eats
or a mouse on a rooftop
with no trap doors,
with nothing more honest
than your hand in her hand—

with nobody, nobody but you!
and all those things.
nobody, nobody but you!
Oh! There is no translating
that ocean,
that music,
that theater,
that field of ponies.

ANNE SEXTON

Twice Shy

Her scarf *à la* Bardot,
In suede flats for the walk,
She came with me one evening
For air and friendly talk.
We crossed the quiet river,
Took the embankment walk.

Traffic holding its breath,
Sky a tense diaphragm:
Dusk hung like a backcloth
That shook where a swan swam,
Tremulous as a hawk
Hanging deadly, calm.

A vacuum of need
Collapsed each hunting heart
But tremulously we held
As hawk and prey apart,
Preserved classic decorum,
Deployed our talk with art.

Our juvenilia
Had taught us both to wait,
Not to publish feeling
And regret it all too late—
Mushroom loves already
Had puffed and burst in hate.

So, chary and excited
As a thrush linked on a hawk,
We thrilled to the March twilight
With nervous childish talk:
Still waters running deep
Along the embankment walk.

SEAMUS HEANEY

On Sweet Killen Hill

AFTER THE IRISH, 18TH CENTURY

Flower of the flock,
Any time, any land,
Plenty your ringlets,
Plenty your hand,
Sunlight your window,
Laughter your sill,
And I must be with you
On sweet Killen Hill.

Let sleep renegue me,
Skin lap my bones,
Love and tomorrow
Can handle the reins.
You my companion
I'd never breathe ill,
And I guarantee bounty
On sweet Killen Hill.

You'll hear the pack yell
As puss devil-dances,
Hear cuckoo and thrush
Pluck song from the branches,
See fish in the pool
Doing their thing,
And the bay as God made it
From sweet Killen Hill.

Pulse of my life,
We come back to—*mise**
Why slave for McArdle
That bumbailiff's issue,
I've harp in a thousand,
Love songs at will,
And the air is cadenza
On sweet Killen Hill.

---

* Gaelic "me," pronounced "mish-e"

Gentle one, lovely one,
Come to me,
Now sleep the clergy,
Now sleep their care,
Sunrise will find us
But sunrise won't tell
That love lacks surveillance
On sweet Killen Hill.

TOM MACINTYRE

A Road in Kentucky

And when that ballad lady went
    to ease the lover whose life she broke,
oh surely this is the road she took,
    road all hackled through barberry fire,
through cedar and alder and sumac and thorn.

Red clay stained her flounces
    and stones cut her shoes
and the road twisted on to his loveless house
    and his cornfield dying
in the scarecrow's arms.

And when she had left her lover lying
    so stark and so stark, with the Star-of-Hope
drawn over his eyes, oh this is the road
    that lady walked in the cawing light,
so dark and so dark in the briary light.

ROBERT HAYDEN

Late Abed

Ah, but a good wife!
To lie late in a warm bed
(warm where she was) with your life
suspended like a music in the head,
hearing her foot in the house, her broom
on the pine floor of the down-stairs room,
hearing the window toward the sun go up,
the tap turned on, the tap turned off,
the saucer clatter to the coffee cup . . .

To lie late in the odor of coffee
thinking of nothing at all, listening . . .

and she moves here, she moves there,
and your mouth hurts still where last she kissed you:
you think how she looked as she left, the bare
thigh, and went to her adorning . . .

You lie there listening and she moves—
prepares her house to hold another morning,
prepares another day to hold her loves . . .

You lie there
thinking of nothing
watching the sky . . .

ARCHIBALD MACLEISH

The First Snow of the Year

The old man, listening to the careful
Steps of his old wife as up she came,
Up, up, so slowly, then her slippered
Progress down the long hall to their door—

Outside the wind, wilder suddenly,
Whirled the first snow of the year; danced
Round and round with it, coming closer
And closer, peppering the panes; now here she was—

Said "Ah, my dear, remember?" But his tray
Took all of her attention, having to hold it
Level. "Ah, my dear, don't you remember?"
"What?" "That time we walked in the white woods."

She handed him his napkin; felt the glass
To make sure the milk in it was warm;
Sat down; got up again; brought comb and brush
To tidy his top hair. "Yes, I remember."

He wondered if she saw now what he did.
Possibly not. An afternoon so windless,
The huge flakes rustled upon each other,
Filling the woods, the world, with cold, cold—

They shivered, having a long way to go,
And then their mittens touched; and touched again;
Their eyes, trying not to meet, did meet;
They stopped, and in the cold held out their arms

Till she came into his; awkwardly,
As girl to boy that never kissed before.
The woods, the darkening world, so cold, so cold,
While these two burned together. He remembered,

And wondered if she did, how like a sting,
A hidden heat it was; while there they stood
And trembled, and the snow made statues of them.
"Ah, my dear, remember?" "Yes, I do."

She rocked and thought: he wants me to say something.
But we said nothing then. The main thing is,
I'm with him still; he calls me and I come.
But slowly. Time makes sluggards of us all.

"Yes, I do remember." The wild wind
Was louder, but a sweetness in her speaking
Stung him, and he heard. While round and round
The first snow of the year danced on the lawn.

MARK VAN DOREN

The
Buzzing
Doubt

The Buzzing Doubt

Now do you suppose that bee
Who bumped the window-pane
Several hard taps with his nose
About two feet short of me
Turned away perfectly sane
To his routine date with the rose—

Or can we imagine a hive
Now host to the buzzing doubt
That things are not what they seem,
That to aim is not to arrive,
Nor the enterer sure to come out,
Nor honey an adequate theme?

DONALD L. HILL

Free Will

As the leaves say
"I'll go this way,
I'll go that way,"
We go these ways

Under the wind.
Soon as we find
We are off and,
Broad as a fen,

Are free, we fold
That way and this,
Testing each wish.
Whether it is

Weal or woe
Do not know,
Simply go.

We go this way
We go that way.
We go these ways.

WALTER CLARK

Will You, Won't You?

Cat in the cold, so eager to come in—
The door opens, and there is no more cat—
Where is he? On the best bed already.
How did he get there in no time at all?

Warm nights, he hesitates; retreats;
Advances; sniffs the threshold, rubs the jamb;
Goes again; returns; stretches his neck
To see what he knows will be there—nothing is strange—

Come in, come in! And so he does. But says:
Doors are final. Have to think them over.
In, out—which is better? Two
Minds about it—mine. Yours, a third.

MARK VAN DOREN

Gulls

The full moon half way up the sky
And Orion hunching in the East
With promise of months of cold and snow,
On a night so still and clear, for all
The brightness of the moon and the stars
Swayed in the water and the back-lit
Islands were deep as the mouths of caves,
There came through the closed windows
And doors, over the minor talk,
A torrent of gulls' cries, wave on wave
Mounting in outrage, horror and despair,
Thousands together.

Their cries like ambulance sirens drew me
Outside and down the hill to the sea-wall
To strain into the darkness until
At last I understood their message:
They had just discovered—who knows how—
The tide was never going out again,
Their favorite flats would be forever
Submerged, and starvation was on its way.

Turns out they were wrong about
The tide, but just because it had
Gone out before was flimsy ground
For hope, especially on such
A night, surrounded by such cries.

E. A. MUIR

Traveling through the Dark

Traveling through the dark I found a deer
dead on the edge of the Wilson River road.
It is usually best to roll them into the canyon:
that road is narrow; to swerve might make more dead.

By glow of the tail-light I stumbled back of the car
and stood by the heap, a doe, a recent killing;
she had stiffened already, almost cold.
I dragged her off; she was large in the belly.

My fingers touching her side brought me the reason—
her side was warm; her fawn lay there waiting,
alive, still, never to be born.
Beside that mountain road I hesitated.

The car aimed ahead its lowered parking lights;
under the hood purred the steady engine.
I stood in the glare of the warm exhaust turning red;
around our group I could hear the wilderness listen.

I thought hard for us all—my only swerving—,
then pushed her over the edge into the river.

WILLIAM STAFFORD

The Peepers in Our Meadow

The way at night these piping peepers
suddenly and all at once are still—
too suddenly, too all together, to have dropped asleep
at God's sweet will.

Things stop like that: altogether.
Nations falter, great art fails,
ages of poetry draw Periclean breath;
then death prevails.

What stills these peepers in our midnight pond?
Do wings go over? Skulkers come?
Or are they silenced by that silence out beyond?
Struck dumb?

ARCHIBALD MACLEISH

The Blue Gift

Is it a dream, or not? During my fever,
For two cold days the wind has
Clawed at the cabin,
Driving and packing the snow
Hard over the land,
Striking the rivers to stone.
In the blizzard, the breath
Of ancient creatures, prowling,
Stalking a glacial dusk.
They bring the gift, the blue gift
Tangled in antlers, the long death
That sleeps in ice,
The seed within the husk.

DAVID PERKINS

John Mouldy

I spied John Mouldy in his cellar,
Deep down twenty steps of stone;
In the dusk he sat a-smiling,
  Smiling there alone.

He read no book, he snuffed no candle;
The rats ran in, the rats ran out;
And far and near, the drip of water
  Went whisp'ring about.

The dusk was still, with dew a-falling,
I saw the Dog-star bleak and grim,
I saw a slim brown rat of Norway
  Creep over him.

I spied John Mouldy in his cellar,
Deep down twenty steps of stone;
In the dusk he sat a-smiling,
  Smiling there alone.

WALTER DE LA MARE

Beyond the Hunting Woods

I speak of that great house
Beyond the hunting woods,
Turreted and towered
In nineteenth-century style,
Where fireflies by the hundreds
Leap in the long grass,
Odor of jessamine
and roses, canker-bit,
Recalling famous times
When dame and maiden sipped
Sassafras or wild
Elderberry wine,
While far in the hunting woods
Men after their red hounds
Pursued the mythic beast.

I ask it of a stranger,
In all that great house finding
Not any living thing,
Or of the wind and the weather,
What charm was in that wine
That they should vanish so,
Ladies in their stiff
Bone and clean of limb,
And over the hunting woods
What mist had maddened them
That gentlemen should lose
Not only the beast in view
But Belle and Ginger too,
Nor home from the hunting woods
Ever, ever come?

DONALD JUSTICE

The Listeners

"Is there anybody there?" said the Traveller,
    Knocking on the moonlit door;
And his horse in the silence champed the grasses
    Of the forest's ferny floor:
And a bird flew up out of the turret,
    Above the Traveller's head:
And he smote upon the door again a second time;
    "Is there anybody there?" he said.
But no one descended to the Traveller;
    No head from the leaf-fringed sill
Leaned over and looked into his grey eyes,
    Where he stood perplexed and still.
But only a host of phantom listeners
    That dwelt in the lone house then
Stood listening in the quiet of the moonlight
    To that voice from the world of men:
Stood thronging the faint moonbeams on the dark stair,
    That goes down to the empty hall,
Hearkening in an air stirred and shaken
    By the lonely Traveller's call.
And he felt in his heart their strangeness,
    Their stillness answering his cry,
While his horse moved, cropping the dark turf,
    'Neath the starred and leafy sky;
For he suddenly smote on the door, even
    Louder, and lifted his head:—
"Tell them I came, and no one answered,
    That I kept my word," he said.
Never the least stir made the listeners,
    Though every word he spake
Fell echoing through the shadowiness of the still house
    From the one man left awake:
Ay, they heard his foot upon the stirrup,
    And the sound of iron on stone,
And how the silence surged softly backward,
    When the plunging hoofs were gone.

WALTER DE LA MARE

Unidentified Flying Object

It's true Mattie Lee
has clean disappeared.
And shouldn't we notify
the sheriff? No use, Will
insists, no earthly use.

He was sleeping one off
under the trees that night,
he claims, and woke up when
the space-ship
landed—a silvery dome

with gassy-green and red-
hot-looking lights like eyes
that stared blinked stared.
Says he hid himself
in the bushes and watched,

shaking. Pretty soon
a hatch slides open, a ramp
glides forward like
a glowing tongue poked out.
And who or what is it

silently present there?
Same as if Will's
trying to peer through webs
and bars of gauzy glare
screening, distorting a shape

he sees yet cannot see.
But crazier than that
was when Mattie Lee
came running from her house
towards the thing.

She's wearing her sunflower hat
and the dress the lady she cooked
for gave her, and it's like
she's late for work the way
she scurries up the ramp.

And it seems to Will
that in its queer
shining, plain Mattie Lee's
transformed—is every teasing brown
he's ever wanted, never had.

He's fixing to shout, Come back,
Mattie Lee, come back;
but a heavy hand is over his mouth
when he hears her laugh
as she steps inside

without even a goodbye glance
around. The next Will knew,
the UFO rose in the air—
no blastoff roar, no flame,
he says—hung in the dark,

hovered, shimmered,
its eyes pulsing, then whirred
spiraling into the sky,
vanished as though
it had never been.

Will's tale anyhow.
All I'm certain of
is Mattie Lee's
nowhere to be found
and must have gone

off in a hurry. Left her doors
unlocked and the radio on
and a roast in the oven. Strange.
As for Will, he's a changed man,
not drinking nowadays and sad.

Mattie Lee's friends—
she's got no kinfolks, lived
alone—are worried, swear
Will was craving her
and she held herself too good

for him, being head of Mount
Nebo's usher board and such.
And some are hinting what I,
for one—well, never mind.
The talk is getting mean.

ROBERT HAYDEN

Taking
Wing

The Morning After

The morning after
　AFTER
The Princess woke
　At 5 a.m.
(Laughter
Of an early rooster
　Broke
The cockles of her dream.)

She felt the pea under the bed,
Corn shucks and straw.

Inside her head
A woodpecker began to tap,
Faster, faster.

She lay still
　And saw
Tomorrows of tomorrow
　Cross the ceiling.

She lay still
　And tried to keep
Inside the story,
　Tried to sleep.

She lay still
　Until
Something rolled over
　Against her shoulder.

"Oh! Oh! Oh!" cried the Princess,
"What was that?"
And she sat right up in bed.

It was the Prince!

He had a face like a dried quince,
A breath like a flying mare,
His hands were red,
His nose was choked with hairy weeds
Out of a flowerpot head.

She wished she were dead.

She tried to remember the Words.
She knew there were Words to be said,
There had to be Words: and Somebody there;
Perhaps out back of the shed.

Inside her head
The woodpecker began to tap
In Morse code.

(Faster, faster.)

"I must be dreaming," she said,
And crawled out of bed.
Her slippers were cold,
The stove wouldn't light
(Something about those slippers
    she had a feeling.)
"The wrong dream," she said,
Heating coffee for the Prince, her master.

WALTER CLARK

The Moon

A woman who lived
in a tree caught
the moon in a kettle.

The wind on the roof
of the tree thumped
while she built her fire.

She boiled it down
to a flat bean
to set on her plate.

She swallowed the moon
and the moon grew
like a child inside her.

When the wind flew away
she mounted
the steps of the air

to bear the moon
on a dark bed
in the house of the night.

She nurses him
while the wind perches
like a heavy bird

in the void branches
of a tree, beside
a cold kettle.

DONALD HALL

Simultaneously

Simultaneously, five thousand miles apart,
two telephone poles, shaking and roaring
and hissing gas, rose from their emplacements
straight up, leveled off and headed
for each other's land, alerted radar
and ground defense, passed each other
in midair, escorted by worried planes,
and plunged into each other's place,
steaming and silent and standing straight,
sprouting leaves.

DAVID IGNATOW

In Memory of the Circus Ship Euzkera, Wrecked in the Caribbean Sea, 1 September 1948

The most stupendous show they ever gave
Must have been that *bizarrerie* of wreck;
The lion tamer spoke from a green wave
And lions slithered slowly off the deck.

Amazing. And the high-wire artists fell
(As we'd all hoped, in secret) through no net
And ten miles down, a plunge they must know well,
And landed soft, and there they're lying yet.

Then, while the brass band played a languid waltz,
The elephant, in pearls and amethysts,
Toppled and turned his ponderous somersaults,
Dismaying some remote geologists.

The tiger followed, and the tiger's mate.
The seals leaped joyful from their brackish tank.
The fortuneteller read the palm of Fate—
Beware of ocean voyages—and sank.

Full fathom five the fattest lady lies,
Among the popcorn and the caged baboons,
And dreams of mermaids' elegant surprise,
To see the bunting and the blue balloons.

WALKER GIBSON

The Mole

Sometimes I envy those
who spring like great black-
and-gold butterflies
before the crowded feet
of summer—
              brief, intense,
like pieces of the sun,
they are remembered and celebrated
long after night has fallen.

But I believe also in one
who in the dead of winter
tunnels through a damp,
clinging darkness,
nosing the soil of old gardens.

He lives unnoticed, but
deep within him there is a dream
of the surface one day
breaking and crumbling:

and a small, brown-furred
figure stands there,
blinking at the sky,
as the rising sun slowly dries
his strange, unruly wings.

JOHN HAINES

Cold Water

I step around a gate of bushes
in the mess
and trickle of a dammed stream
and my shoe fills with cold water. I
enter the shade
of a thicket, a black pool,
a small circle of stunned drowsing air,

vaulted with birch which meets overhead
as if smoke
rose up and turned into leaves.
I stand on the roots of a maple
and imagine dropping a line. My wrist jumps
with the pain of a live mouth hooked deep,

and I stare, and watch where the lithe stripe
tears water.
Then it heaves on my hand: cold,
squaretailed, flecked, revenant flesh
of a Brook Trout.
The pine forests I walked through
darken and cool a dead farmer's brook.

I look up and see the Iroquois
coming back
standing among the birches
on the other side of the black pool.

The five elders
have come for me, I am young,
my naked body whitens with cold

in the snow, blisters in the bare sun,
the ice cuts
me, the thorns of blackberries:
I am ready for the mystery.
I follow them
over the speechless needles
of pines which are dead or born again.

DONALD HALL

If the Owl Calls Again

at dusk
from the island in the river,
and it's not too cold,

I'll wait for the moon
to rise,
then take wing and glide
to meet him.

We will not speak,
but hooded against the frost
soar above
the alder flats, searching
with tawny eyes.

And then we'll sit
in the shadowy spruce and
pick the bones
of careless mice,

while the long moon drifts
toward Asia
and the river mutters
in its icy bed.

And when morning climbs
the limbs
we'll part without a sound,

fulfilled, floating
homeward as
the cold world wakens.

JOHN HAINES

Night Crow

When I saw that clumsy crow
Flap from a wasted tree,
A shape in the mind rose up:
Over the gulfs of dream
Flew a tremendous bird
Further and further away
Into a moonless black,
Deep in the brain, far back.

THEODORE ROETHKE

The Thought-Fox

I imagine this midnight moment's forest:
Something else is alive
Beside the clock's loneliness
And this blank page where my fingers move.

Through the window I see no star:
Something more near
Though deeper within darkness
Is entering the loneliness:

Cold, delicately at the dark snow
A fox's nose touches twig, leaf;
Two eyes serve a movement, that now
And again now, and now, and now

Sets neat prints into the snow
Between trees, and warily a lame
Shadow lags by stump and in hollow
Of a body that is bold to come

Across clearings, an eye,
A widening deepening greenness,
Brilliantly, concentratedly,
Coming about its own business

Till, with a sudden sharp hot stink of fox,
It enters the dark hole of the head.
The window is starless still; the clock ticks,
The page is printed.

TED HUGHES

The Heaven of Animals

Here they are. The soft eyes open.
If they have lived in a wood
It is a wood.
If they have lived on plains
It is grass rolling
Under their feet forever.

Having no souls, they have come,
Anyway, beyond their knowing.
Their instincts wholly bloom
And they rise.
The soft eyes open.

To match them, the landscape flowers,
Outdoing, desperately
Outdoing what is required:
The richest wood,
The deepest field.

For some of these,
It could not be the place
It is, without blood.
These hunt, as they have done,
But with claws and teeth grown perfect,

More deadly than they can believe.
They stalk more silently,
And crouch on the limbs of trees,
And their descent
Upon the bright backs of their prey

May take years
In a sovereign floating of joy.
And those that are hunted
Know this as their life,
Their reward: to walk

Under such trees in full knowledge
Of what is in glory above them,
And to feel no fear,
But acceptance, compliance.
Fulfilling themselves without pain

At the cycle's center,
They tremble, they walk
Under the tree,
They fall, they are torn,
They rise, they walk again.

JAMES DICKEY

*That
Dark
Other
Mountain*

Incident in a Rose Garden

A VARIATION ON AN
OLD THEME, FOR M.S.

Gardener: Sir, I encountered Death
Just now among our roses.
Thin as a scythe he stood there.

I knew him by his pictures.
He had his black coat on,
Black gloves, a broad black hat.

I think he would have spoken,
Seeing his mouth stood open.
Big it was, with white teeth.

As soon as he beckoned, I ran.
I ran until I found you.
Sir, I am quitting my job.

I want to see my sons
Once more before I die.
I want to see California.

Master: Sir, you must be that stranger
Who threatened my gardener.
This is my property, sir.

I welcome only friends here.
Death: Sir, I knew your father.
And we were friends at the end.

As for your gardener,
I did not threaten him.
Old men mistake my gestures.

I only meant to ask him
To show me to his master.
I take it you are he?

DONALD JUSTICE

A Broken Gull

Denied the shelter of air and the power
Of water, this poor creature called all night
And carved a voice of pain in my dreams.
With eyes whetted keen in my dream
I saw once more the gull, lopsided
And broken like a used-up toy,
Turn circles at the water-edge on
One foot, probing her soft head and beak
To quest out the injury, and failing,
Stop to turn the glazed eye of pain
On me who stood there,
The source of help, yet unable to act.

The first light found her dead,
A wrinkled shape of dirty white
Like paper crumpled up and
Thrown away, but for her beak,
Half open in a soundless call.

Now, why must this death catch me so sorely,
Who have no claims but sentiment to hold me here?

                             Still,
I know I shall wake to many nights
With this bereavement troubling me.

JOHN MOORE

The Early Purges

I was six when I first saw kittens drown.
Dan Taggart pitched them, "the scraggy wee shits,"
Into a bucket; a frail metal sound,

Soft paws scraping like mad. But their tiny din
Was soon soused. They were slung on the snout
Of the pump and the water pumped in.

"Sure isn't it better for them now?" Dan said.
Like wet gloves they bobbed and shone till he sluiced
Them out on the dunghill, glossy and dead.

Suddenly frightened, for days I sadly hung
Round the yard, watching the three sogged remains
Turn mealy and crisp as old summer dung

Until I forgot them. But the fear came back
When Dan trapped big rats, snared rabbits, shot crows
Or, with a sickening tug, pulled old hens' necks.

Still, living displaces false sentiments
And now, when shrill pups are prodded to drown
I just shrug, "Bloody pups." It makes sense:

"Prevention of cruelty" talk cuts ice in town
Where they consider death unnatural,
But on well-run farms pests have to be kept down.

SEAMUS HEANEY

On the Death of Friends in Childhood

We shall not ever meet them bearded in heaven,
Nor sunning themselves among the bald of hell;
If anywhere, in the deserted schoolyard at twilight,
Forming a ring, perhaps, or joining hands
In games whose very names we have forgotten.
Come, memory, let us seek them there in the shadows.

DONALD JUSTICE

Little Elegy

FOR A CHILD WHO SKIPPED ROPE

Here lies resting, out of breath,
Out of turns, Elizabeth
Whose quicksilver toes not quite
Cleared the whirring edge of night.

Earth whose circles round us skim
Till they catch the lightest limb,
Shelter now Elizabeth
And for her sake trip up Death.

X. J. KENNEDY

First Death in Nova Scotia

In the cold, cold parlor
my mother laid out Arthur
beneath the chromographs:
Edward, Prince of Wales,
with Princess Alexandra,
and King George with Queen Mary.
Below them on the table
stood a stuffed loon
shot and stuffed by Uncle
Arthur, Arthur's father.

Since Uncle Arthur fired
a bullet into him,
he hadn't said a word.
He kept his own counsel
on his white, frozen lake,
the marble-topped table.
His breast was deep and white,
cold and caressable;
his eyes were red glass,
much to be desired.

"Come," said my mother,
"Come and say goodbye
to your little cousin Arthur."
I was lifted up and given
one lily of the valley
to put in Arthur's hand.
Arthur's coffin was
a little frosted cake,
and the red-eyed loon eyed it
from his white, frozen lake.

Arthur was very small.
He was all white, like a doll
that hadn't been painted yet.
Jack Frost had started to paint him
the way he always painted
the Maple Leaf (Forever).
He had just begun on his hair,

a few red strokes, and then
Jack Frost had dropped the brush
and left him white, forever.

The gracious royal couples
were warm in red and ermine;
their feet were well wrapped up
in the ladies' ermine trains.
They invited Arthur to be
the smallest page at court.
But how could Arthur go,
clutching his tiny lily,
with his eyes shut up so tight
and the roads deep in snow?

ELIZABETH BISHOP

Mid-Term Break

I sat all morning in the college sick bay
Counting bells knelling classes to a close.
At two o'clock our neighbours drove me home.

In the porch I met my father crying—
He had always taken funerals in his stride—
And Big Jim Evans saying it was a hard blow.

The baby cooed and laughed and rocked the pram
When I came in, and I was embarrassed
By old men standing up to shake my hand

And tell me they were "sorry for my trouble,"
Whispers informed strangers I was the eldest,
Away at school, as my mother held my hand

In hers and coughed out angry tearless sighs.
At ten o'clock the ambulance arrived
With the corpse, stanched and bandaged by the nurses.

Next morning I went up into the room. Snowdrops
And candles soothed the bedside; I saw him
For the first time in six weeks. Paler now,

Wearing a poppy bruise on his left temple,
He lay in his four foot box as in his cot.
No gaudy scars, the bumper knocked him clear.

A four foot box, a foot for every year.

SEAMUS HEANEY

The Lesson

"Your father's gone," my bald headmaster said.
His shiny dome and brown tobacco jar
Splintered at once in tears. It wasn't grief.
I cried for knowledge which was bitterer
Than any grief. For there and then I knew
That grief has uses—that a father dead
Could bind the bully's fist a week or two;
And then I cried for shame, then for relief.

I was a month past ten when I learnt this:
I still remember how the noise was stilled
In school-assembly when my grief came in.
Some goldfish in a bowl quietly sculled
Around their shining prison on its shelf.
They were indifferent. All the other eyes
Were turned toward me. Somewhere in myself
Pride, like a goldfish, flashed a sudden fin.

EDWARD LUCIE-SMITH

That Dark Other Mountain

My father could go down a mountain faster than I
Though I was first one up.
Legs braced or with quick steps he slid the gravel slopes
Where I picked cautious footholds.

Black, Iron, Eagle, Doublehead, Chocorua,
Wildcat and Carter Dome—
He beat me down them all. And that last other mountain,
And that dark other mountain.

ROBERT FRANCIS

Angina Pectoris

The steady heart, which in its steadiness
Allows formation of the somewhat, life,
Unsteadies, stops, and so a thick debris
Drops to the sidewalk, where the poor limbs sprawl
Like things a child had made of mud, and all
The color leaves the face, pale as a knife.

When the man walked down the street in his mackinaw,
Or sat in a barroom gurgling at his beer,
It was only a small usurper of oxygen
I noticed; I'd have seen him ship for Spain,
Or go to Dakota and die working with grain,
And never thought, or been glad he was not here.

But now that I see him neutral earth, to bury
In earth, for damp, or a pale, poetic swarm
Of worms to end, I'm sorry; I wish him what
I'd not wish other mud: that he ate tonight
With children he loved, that the meal was heavy and right,
That he slept with plenty of quilts to keep him warm.

W. R. MOSES

The Death of the Craneman

Happened like this: it was hot as hell
That afternoon, sand, stone dust, the sun,
We were in the mountains.
Drinking-water was by the gasoline drum,
We were all drinking like fish that day.
He must have come down from the crane
For a drink I guess, a cigarette
Might have done it, blew it bang up, that drum.
Like dynamite been dropped in it.
We came running down from the mountains.

The blacksmith got to him first: gasoline
Had made a bonfire of him, and we shouted
Craneman! Craneman! with the wops talking
Their language, and nobody knowing his name.
Standing there you could see him, a flame
Lighter and yellower than the sunlight,
And burning, hands and feet, his hair on fire,
Getting up from the ground, standing there,
Yelling out of the fire, flame shooting white
In the sunlight: Lemme alone! Lemme alone!
I'm all right!

Well, we get him here and here he dies.
And that's where we buried him out there,
In the goldenrod beyond them pines.
It's a Potter's Field and nobody'd care.
We dug the grave with our drills and hands.
You got to bury a guy somewhere.
Funny I thought as I looked at him
Blackened, with a pair of holes for eyes,
You bury a stiff and there he lies,
And Christ only knows where he come from
And whether there's kids somewhere or a dame,
We buried him like he came in this world,
A stiff, naked, without a name.

ALFRED HAYES

244

A Woman Mourned
by Daughters

Now, not a tear begun,
we sit here in your kitchen,
spent, you see, already.
You are swollen till you strain
this house and the whole sky.
You, whom we so often
succeeded in ignoring!
You are puffed up in death
like a corpse pulled from the sea;
we groan beneath your weight.
And yet you were a leaf,
a straw blown on the bed,
you had long since become
crisp as a dead insect.
What is it, if not you,
that settles on us now
like satin you pulled down
over our bridal heads?
What rises in our throats
like food you prodded in?
Nothing could be enough.
You breathe upon us now
through solid assertions
of yourself: teaspoons, goblets,
seas of carpet, a forest
of old plants to be watered,
an old man in an adjoining
room to be touched and fed.
And all this universe
dares us to lay a finger
anywhere, save exactly
as you would wish it done.

ADRIENNE RICH

Letter from a Death Bed

This afternoon, darling, when you were here,
I meant to say some true and final thing
and could not. I am not all myself
but a chemical changeling, a tide of salt and juices,
a shore from which I sink, wash back, and sink.

Then in a rhythm and for an interval
I am again. I know then—now—exactly
what was my best. That instant—this—I seize,
which is no memory but the being again. At last,
for this instant, I can say "I love you."

I have it here: that first night and the first
again, and always, incredibly—thank you—the first
from the instant of your turning, your dropped silks
a froth at your feet, and like a grained flame
the leap and repose of your nakedness in its giving.

Let the tide wash that from me if it can.
A dark like your body's fuzzes and crinkles takes me.
Then blanks. But is always the last of me.
The last of me going from me is you. And returns.
Goes and returns. Goes and returns. Holding you.

No, I am all going. All arrows set from the wind.
All out and away. Skewed only by cheer and nurses.
Damn them, I will die in my own climate.
What breath have I ever drawn from the wax-weathers
under their hothouse skulls and fogged windows?

I tend a refusal better than their prayers,
these flour-faced angels with their piano legs
who don't think I notice. Today that doctor,
his smile put on with adhesive tape, came poking:
He'll have me out of here in nothing flat.

I know damn well he will. Nothing and flat.
He wants to know my religion. "Refusal," I tell him.
"The Church of the First Covenant of Damned-if-I-Will."
Fool. Does he think what a man lives by
gets changed by his dying? Well, I'm cantankerous—

must I *like* dying to gossip?—Oh, I hear them:
"Twelve, he's a queer one. Won't be told what's wrong.
Just doesn't want to know." I know all right.
If they think what I'm dying of's any one thing,
they haven't healing enough to mend a rip.

. . . What was it I said? "Some true and final thing."
I meant a better end to that beginning.
Well, maybe cantankerousness is true and final.
—No. No, it isn't. Your eyes are true and final.
Your smile even in pity and enforced. Your hand . . .

Thank you for smiling, darling. Don't come back.
Come bury the bones. Come take away the clothes rack
they'll hang my tatters on. But the end's here.
This is my last stroke as myself. My going.
My meat has this last energy and no more—

to praise you as you are from all I leave.

JOHN CIARDI

Burial

Aloft, lightly on fingertips
As crewmen carry a racing shell—
But I was lighter than any shell or ship.

An easy trophy, they picked me up and bore me,
Four of them, an even four.
I knew the pulse and impulse of those hands,

And heard the talking, laughing. I heard
As from an adjoining room, the door ajar,
Voices but not words.

If I am dead (I said)
If this is death,
How casual, how delicate its masque and myth.

One pall bearer, the tenor, spoke,
Another whistled softly, and I tried to smile.
Death? Music? Or a joke?

But still the hands were there.
I rode half on the hands and half in air.
Their strength was equal to my strangeness.

Whatever they do (I said) will be done right,
Whether in earth and dark or in deep light,
Whatever the hands do will be well.

Suddenly I tried to breathe and cry:
Before you put me down, before
I finally die,

Take from the filing folders of my brain
All that is finished or begun—
Then I remembered that this had been done.

So we went on, on
To our party-parting on the hill
Of the blue breath, gray boulder, and my burial.

ROBERT FRANCIS

Nightmares

beware: do not read this poem

tonite, *thriller* was
abt an ol woman, so vain she
surrounded herself w/
    many mirrors

it got so bad that finally she
locked herself indoors & her
whole life became the
   mirrors

one day the villagers broke
into her house, but she was too
swift for them. she disappeared
    into a mirror

each tenant who bought the house
after that, lost a loved one to
    the ol woman in the mirror:
    first a little girl
    then a young woman
    then the young woman/s husband

the hunger of this poem is legendary
it has taken in many victims
back off from this poem
it has drawn in yr feet
back off from this poem
it has drawn in yr legs

back off from this poem
it is a greedy mirror
you are into this poem. from
    the waist down
nobody can hear you can they?
this poem has had you up to here
    belch
this poem aint got no manners
you cant call out frm this poem

relax now & go w/ this poem
move & roll on to this poem
do not resist this poem
this poem has yr eyes
this poem has his head
this poem has his arms
this poem has his fingers
this poem has his fingertips

this poem is the reader & the
reader this poem

statistic: the us bureau of missing persons reports
that in 1968 over 100,000 people disappeared
leaving no solid clues
        nor trace   only
a space   in the lives of their friends

ISHMAEL REED

Was a Man

Was a man, was a two-
faced man, pretended
he wasn't who he was,
who, in a men's room,
faced his hung-over
face in a mirror hung
over the towel rack.
The mirror was cracked.
Shaving close in that
looking glass, he nicked
his throat, bled blue
blood, grabbed a new
towel to patch the wrong
scratch, knocked off
the mirror and, facing
himself, almost intact,
in final terror hung
the wrong face back.

PHILIP BOOTH

compozishun—to james herndon and others

you a man, man, man, who know the other word
and says it like it is

the participle mamma gonnagonget the english teach
in his unsleep at night

the biglegs gonna wrap you hands behine you back
ansnag you feet
the peach-fuzz
watermelon heads
is gonna butt you in the belly

no matter, you pillow head
you know the snakes and hippos gonnakum
is why you guts is dizzy like you gonna fall

some blackmanholecover dont end
like bunnychasincarrot in the zoo
anyou is just a man, man,
is all that you can do

you know, the fruitbowl anall is a lie,
sumpen the head make up for show—
you know, the kids break pencilpoints anleave
the sheet of paper white as snow—you know,
the reason because they just like skate:
he shh at somen that get in the way of the way he wanttgo

they not poor, man, like you or me
they speak s v o
only *their* mammas has *no* strings
—whoooo-eee!—

when the beer wears off
alls you got is you self, man,
like any other man,
analls they got is a tribe, man,
the way they spoze to be

but you man, man,
the way *you* spoze to be

RONALD J. GOBA

The Bird of Night

A shadow is floating through the moonlight,
Its wings don't make a sound.
Its claws are long, its beak is bright.
Its eyes try all the corners of the night.

It calls and calls: all the air swells and heaves
And washes up and down like water.
The ear that listens to the owl believes
In death. The bat beneath the eaves,

The mouse beside the stone are still as death—
The owl's air washes them like water.
The owl goes back and forth inside the night,
And the night holds its breath.

RANDALL JARRELL

An Advancement of Learning

I took the embankment path
(As always, deferring
The bridge). The river nosed past,
Pliable, oil-skinned, wearing

A transfer of gables and sky.
Hunched over the railing,
Well away from the road now, I
Considered the dirty-keeled swans.

Something slobbered curtly, close,
Smudging the silence: a rat
Slimed out of the water and
My throat sickened so quickly that

I turned down the path in cold sweat
But God, another was nimbling
Up the far bank, tracing its wet
Arcs on the stones. Incredibly then

I established a dreaded
Bridgehead. I turned to stare
With deliberate, thrilled care
At my hitherto snubbed rodent.

He clockworked aimlessly a while,
Stopped, back bunched and glistening,
Ears plastered down on his knobbed skull,
Insidiously listening.

The tapered tail that followed him,
The raindrop eye, the old snout:
One by one I took all in.
He trained on me. I stared him out

Forgetting how I used to panic
When his grey brothers scraped and fed
Behind the hen-coop in our yard,
On ceiling boards above my bed.

This terror, cold, wet-furred, small-clawed,
Retreated up a pipe for sewage.
I stared a minute after him.
Then I walked on and crossed the bridge.

SEAMUS HEANEY

Pike

Pike, three inches long, perfect
Pike in all parts, green tigering the gold.
Killers from the egg: the malevolent aged grin.
They dance on the surface among the flies.

Or move, stunned by their own grandeur,
Over a bed of emerald, silhouette
Of submarine delicacy and horror.
A hundred feet long in their world.

In ponds, under the heat-struck lily pads—
Gloom of their stillness:
Logged on last year's black leaves, watching upwards.
Or hung in an amber cavern of weeds.

The jaws' hooked clamp and fangs
Not to be changed at this date;
A life subdued to its instrument;
The gills kneading quietly, and the pectorals.

Three we kept behind glass,
Jungled in weed: three inches, four,
And four and a half: fed fry to them—
Suddenly there were two. Finally one

With a sag belly and the grin it was born with.
And indeed they spare nobody.
Two, six pounds each, over two feet long,
High and dry and dead in the willow-herb—

One jammed past its gills down the other's gullet:
The outside eye stared: as a vise locks—
The same iron in this eye
Though its film shrank in death.

A pond I fished, fifty yards across,
Whose lilies and muscular tench
Had outlasted every visible stone
Of the monastery that planted them—

Stilled legendary depth:
It was as deep as England. It held
Pike too immense to stir, so immense and old
That past nightfall I dared not cast

But silently cast and fished
With the hair frozen on my head
For what might move, for what eye might move.
The still splashes on the dark pond,

Owls hushing the floating woods
Frail on my ear against the dream
Darkness beneath night's darkness had freed,
That rose slowly toward me, watching.

TED HUGHES

Death of a Naturalist

All year the flax-dam festered in the heart
Of the townland; green and heavy headed
Flax had rotted there, weighted down by huge sods.
Daily it sweltered in the punishing sun.
Bubbles gargled delicately, bluebottles
Wove a strong gauze of sound around the smell.
There were dragon-flies, spotted butterflies,
But best of all was the warm thick slobber
Of frogspawn that grew like clotted water
In the shade of the banks. Here, every spring
I would fill jampotfuls of the jellied
Specks to range on window-sills at home,
On shelves at school, and wait and watch until
The fattening dots burst into nimble-
Swimming tadpoles. Miss Walls would tell us how
The daddy frog was called a bullfrog
And how he croaked and how the mammy frog
Laid hundreds of little eggs and this was
Frogspawn. You could tell the weather by frogs too
For they were yellow in the sun and brown
In rain.

Then one hot day when fields were rank
With cowdung in the grass the angry frogs
Invaded the flax-dam; I ducked through hedges
To a coarse croaking that I had not heard
Before. The air was thick with a bass chorus.
Right down the dam gross-bellied frogs were cocked
On sods; their loose necks pulsed like sails. Some hopped:
The slap and plop were obscene threats. Some sat
Poised like mud grenades, their blunt heads farting.
I sickened, turned, and ran. The great slime kings
Were gathered there for vengeance and I knew
That if I dipped my hand the spawn would clutch it.

SEAMUS HEANEY

To Nowhere

I carry my keys like a weapon
their points bunched together
and held outwards in the palm
for a step too close behind me
as I approach the subway through the dark.
Drunks are swaying against walls,
hopped-up men are leaning over
and dancing together crazily
and clapping hands, their faces twitching.
Quiet ones lounge against the wall watching.
They look for the weakness
in a man where they can jump him
and my keys are a sure sign.
I walk as I always do, quickly,
my face set straight ahead
as I pretend not to see or hear,
busy on a mission to nowhere.

DAVID IGNATOW

The Nature of Jungles

Every day, walking the city streets,
He conned within himself the nature of jungles,
Enlarged his mind for poisonous thorns and flies,
And green mambas secret in green tangles.

Under his eyes, vultures degraded death,
And noosing lianas flourished by strangulation;
The worms and shrews under the endless muck
Ate each other in endless repetition.

Every day he perused the paradox,
What grisly fashion life with life mingles;
And saw the teeth that shone for his jugular
Every day, walking the city jungles.

W. R. MOSES

"It Out-Herods Herod.
Pray You, Avoid It."

Tonight my children hunch
Toward their Western, and are glad
As, with a Sunday punch,
The Good casts out the Bad.

And in their fairy tales
The warty giant and witch
Get sealed in doorless jails
And the match-girl strikes it rich.

I've made myself a drink.
The giant and witch are set
To bust out of the clink
When my children have gone to bed.

All frequencies are loud
With signals of despair;
In flash and morse they crowd
The rondure of the air.

For the wicked have grown strong,
Their numbers mock at death,
Their cow brings forth its young,
Their bull engendereth.

Their very fund of strength,
Satan, bestrides the globe;
He stalks its breadth and length
And finds out even Job.

Yet by quite other laws
My children make their case;
Half God, half Santa Claus,
But with my voice and face,

A hero comes to save
The poorman, beggarman, thief,
And make the world behave
And put an end to grief.

And that their sleep be sound
I say this childermas
Who could not, at one time,
Have saved them from the gas.

ANTHONY HECHT

Black Humor

The jangle of the jeering crows
has somehow crossed into my dream
to scream and circle there. I seem
in sleep to understand the crows.

Evil is in the world, they scream.
Something on the garden path
salt as blood and cold as death
has fallen from the air, the dream.

I find it with the daylight, too:
cold upon the path, to gather
drops of silence from the dew,
one inscrutable, black, bleeding feather.

ARCHIBALD MACLEISH

If It Comes

If it comes
to that, go
to bed late,
so, if you
have to wait
without sleep,
you can see
the luminous
dial, and keep
watch on your
self-winding
pulse. Words bug
the least light,
and full-moon
animals, out
to shuttle
the dark, drag
a trapped leg
through the rose
bed. Last night
was the same:
the same noise,
the slow night-
lock rattle,
and no one
there. Finding
yourself where
bat wings swim
the blank sky,
where owls dive
to echo
your own dark
question, yes,
you must go
to bed late:
so, if for

once, you have
enough warning,
enough to break
out, from what
pass as dreams,
you will wake,
if it comes,
near morning.

PHILIP BOOTH

Twilight at the Zoo

The great wrought-iron gates have been
closed for some time now;
no one ever comes.
Only the rimed and bloodshot eye
of late October pierces their detentive tracery
as now, at sunset
when the noises start.

Something
is not as it should be, something
has happened that we do not understand.
Only this morning a cuticle of ice
affronted the flamingoes mincing to the pool
to bathe their nightlong aching feet
and no one came to break it.
We seldom see the keepers. When
we do they are invariably drunk
and do not feed us at the proper times
or with the proper food. Often they do not
feed us at all.

That is the least of it.
Two nights ago a mountain wolf came
slavering around the wire and killed two Chinese geese.
Their feathers are still sticking to the path.

As dusk falls
chill upon cage and compound
the noises begin. These are never
the commonplaces of bank-holiday afternoons
blending on the hot and musky air
with the child's wonder and the parents' platitudes—
the hoarse jokes of the seals, the ribald
whooping of the sycophant hyenas
or the patrician outrage of
peacocks feigning a distaste for being seen.

No. Lately the nights have been
scored with sly crepitations, shrieks
stifled before they break against the bars
and the whispering fury of embattled wings.

First light brings silence
and a perspective of mangled pelts and plumage,
muzzles and beaks dumbstruck with stiffening blood.

Twice now at full moon
the sound of muted chanting has been heard
from the direction of the Baboon Rock
ending each time with the same coda
of screams that mount into a glutted silence.

We no longer dare
count the familiar faces of the keepers.
Worst of all the silence
of the great cats in their pens under the rock-face.
Their nightly grumblings and their morning coughs
were somehow reassuring.
This dreadful silence does not comfort us.
How do we know they are safe inside?

Some of the higher apes
recently spread a rumour that the Director
died many months ago.
They themselves have been accused of mutiny
and the forcing of cages during the hours of darkness.
Macaws and motley cockatoos
rage at us all, night and day,
in a Babel of moulting contradiction.

I had not meant
to cause alarm by telling the whole truth
but these are facts.
Our cages stink.

Many are moping to death.
Marauding bands of chimpanzees and mandrills
parade the avenues in looted uniforms.
They lynched the Fellows in the Orangery.

Under the skeletal beeches on the hill
the blameless deer look upward in their hunger.
It is not manna
falls on them from these livid clouds.

ALEX RODGER

Love Song for the Future

To our ruined vineyard come,
Little foxes, for your share
Of our blighted grapes, the tomb
Readied for our common lair.
Ants, we open you the cupboard;
Flee no more the heavy hand
Harmless as a vacant scabbard
Since our homes like yours are sand.

Catamounts so often hunted,
Wend your ways through town or city,
Since both you and we are haunted
By the Weird Ones with no pity.
Deer and bear we used to stalk,
We would spend our dying pains
Nestling you with mouse and hawk
Near our warmth until it wanes.

Weave across our faces, spiders,
Webwork fragile as a flower;
Welcome, serpents, subtle gliders,
For your poison fails in power.
Loathed no longer, learn your worth,
Toad and lizard, snail and eel—
Remnants of a living earth
Cancelled by a world of steel,

Whose miasmic glitter dances
Over beast's and man's sick daze
While our eyes which scorned St. Francis
Watch Isaiah's vision craze:
Ox and lion mingling breath
Eat the straw of doom; in tether
To the selfsame stake of death
Wolf and lamb lie down together.

VASSAR MILLER

The End of the World

Quite unexpectedly as Vasserot
The armless ambidextrian was lighting
A match between his great and second toe
And Ralph the lion was engaged in biting
The neck of Madame Sossman while the drum
Pointed, and Teeny was about to cough
In waltz-time swinging Jocko by the thumb—
Quite unexpectedly the top blew off:

And there, there overhead, there, there, hung over
Those thousands of white faces, those dazed eyes,
There in the starless dark the poise, the hover,
There with vast wings across the canceled skies,
There in the sudden blackness the black pall
Of nothing, nothing, nothing—nothing at all.

ARCHIBALD MACLEISH

Barker, George, 43
Bishop, Elizabeth, 37, 118, 156, 238
Bly, Robert, 74, 88, 170
Booth, Philip, 4, 253, 266
Burr, Gray, 162

Ciardi, John, 50, 246
Clark, Walter, 31, 62, 204, 219
Clifton, Lucille, 6
Cummings, E. E., 11, 32, 57, 85, 190

de la Mare, Walter, 171, 210, 213
Dickey, James, 229
Donnelly, Dorothy, 7, 99, 109, 134, 173
Dugan, Alan, 41

Finkel, Donald, 80
Fletcher, John Gould, 128
Francis, Robert, 5, 20, 24, 26, 147, 242, 248
Frost, Robert, 49, 111, 169, 176

Gibson, Walker, 223
Goba, Ronald J., 254
Graves, Robert, 59

Haines, John, 86, 109, 224, 226
Hall, Donald, 136, 154, 221, 225
Hayden, Robert, 16, 34, 93, 164, 196, 214
Hayes, Alfred, 244
Heaney, Seamus, 9, 121, 193, 235, 240, 256, 260
Hecht, Anthony, 52, 264
Hill, Donald L., 203
Howes, Barbara, 71, 140
Hughes, Ted, 228, 258

Ignatow, David, 222, 262

Jarrell, Randall, 79, 255
Justice, Donald, 3, 33, 119, 152, 212, 233, 236

Kennedy, X. J., 159, 237
Kinnell, Galway, 8

Lake, Richard, 129
Larkin, 83
Lee, Laurie, 91, 101
Lipsitz, Lou, 76, 84, 165
Logan, John, 187
Lucie-Smith, Edward, 241

MacIntyre, Tom, 194
MacLeish, Archibald, 88, 103, 105, 123, 146, 177, 197, 208, 265, 272
Miles, Josephine, 54
Miller, Vassar, 69, 115, 151, 271
Moore, John, 70, 120, 234
Moore, Marianne, 65
Morrison, Lillian, 23
Moses, W. R., 25, 68, 102, 104, 243, 263
Muir, E. A., 206

Nathan, Leonard, 35
Nemerov, Howard, 124, 144, 158
Nowlan, Alden, 160

Perkins, David, 45, 181, 209
Plath, Sylvia, 133, 135

Randall, Dudley, 189
Ransom, John Crowe, 137
Reed, Ishmael, 251

Reid, Alastair, 141
Rich, Adrienne, 39, 153, 245
Rodger, Alex, 268
Roethke, Theodore, 10, 14, 42,
    43, 122, 126, 145, 227

Sandburg, Carl, 172
Sarton, May, 91
Scannell, Vernon, 21
Sexton, Anne, 40, 163, 191
Shapiro, Karl, 66
Smith, William Jay, 108
Snodgrass, W. D., 72, 138
Snyder, Gary, 75, 94
Spacks, Barry, 73
Stafford, William, 155, 207
Starbuck, George, 55
Stephens, James, 58

Stevens, Wallace, 117
Stevenson, Anne, 19, 67, 100, 185

Thomas, D. M., 182
Thomas, Edward, 130
Trypanis, C. A., 51

Van Doren, Mark, 116, 176, 184,
    198, 205

Whittemore, Reed, 53, 56, 110,
    139
Wilbur, Richard, 22, 27, 44, 77,
    78, 89, 92, 95, 139, 157, 161
Williams, William Carlos, 15,
    84, 102, 107
Wolfe, Thomas, 36, 87
Wright, Judith, 174

Advancement of Learning, An, 256
After Rain, 130
After Snow, 31
And When the Green Man Comes, 86
Angina Pectoris, 243
Atavism, 129

Balloons, 135
Base Stealer, The, 24
Bears, 153
Ben, 36
beware: do not read this poem, 251
Beyond the Hunting Woods, 212
Big Wind, 122
Bird of Night, The, 255
Blackberry Sweet, 189
Black Humor, 265
Black November Turkey, A, 78
Blue Gift, The, 209
Boy in the Roman Zoo, 177
Brainstorm, 124
Broken Gull, A, 234
Burial, 248
buy me an ounce and i'll sell you a pound, 11
Buzzing Doubt, The, 203

Catch, 26
Cat on Couch, 71
Child, The, 136
Child at Winter Sunset, The, 176
Child on Top of a Greenhouse, 145
Chinese Baby Asleep, 134
Chipmunk's Day, The, 79
Cold Water, 225

compozishun—to james herndon and others, 254
Cora Punctuated with Strawberries, 55

Daedalus, 141
Dance, The, 15
Death of a Naturalist, 260
Death of the Craneman, The, 244
Desert Places, 111
Digging for China, 157
Dingman's Marsh, 70
Driving Toward the Lac Qui Parle River, 74

Early Purges, The, 235
Early Supper, 140
Eden, 182
Egrets, 174
Elegy, 42
Eleven, 146
End of the World, The, 272
Exeunt, 95

Falling in Love, 181
Farm, The, 69
Farm Boy After Summer, 147
Field of Autumn, 101
Fire-Truck, A, 77
First Confession, 159
First Death in Nova Scotia, 238
First Sight, 83
First Song, 8
First Snow of the Year, The, 198
Free Will, 204
From "Heart's Needle," 138

Given Note, The, 9
Glass of Beer, A, 58

Glass World, 109
Good Times, 6
Grandfathers, The, 33
Gulls, 206

Harbor, The, 172
Heaven of Animals, The, 229
He Was, 44
High School Band, The, 53
House Guest, 37
"How Long Hast Thou Been A
    Gravemaker?", 45
Hunting Song, 80
Hurricane, 123

I, Icarus, 160
If It Comes, 266
If the Owl Calls Again, 226
Impulse of October, The, 102
Incident in a Rose Garden, 233
Indian Summer: Vermont, 100
in Just-, 85
In Memory of the Circus Ship
    Euzkera, 223
Invocation, 151
"It Out-Herods Herod. Pray
    You, Avoid It," 264

Janet Waking, 137
John Mouldy, 210
Juggler, 22

Kid, 34
King Wind, 116

Late Abed, 197
Late Spring Day in My Life, A,
    88
Leaflight, 99
Lesson, The, 241
Letter fom a Death Bed, 246
Listeners, The, 213

Little Elegy, 237
Little Exercise, 118
Little-League Baseball Fan, 25
Lizards and Snakes, 52
Lobsters in the Window, 72
Local Storm, A, 119
Love, 185
Love Song, 191
Love Song for the Future, 271

Manhole Covers, 66
Manners, 156
March (I), 84
Memory of a Porch, 152
Mid-August at Sourdough Moun-
    tain Lookout, 94
Mid-Term Break, 240
Mind, 27
Mole, The, 224
Moon, The, 221
Morning After, The, 219
Mousemeal, 144
Mouse Night: One of Our
    Games, 155
My Father Paints the Summer,
    92
My Papa's Waltz, 14

Nature of Jungles, The, 263
"next to of course god america i,
    57
Night Crow, 227
Night Wind in Fall, 104
Niño Leading an Old Man to
    Market, 35
Nothing Gold Can Stay, 169

O Daedalus, Fly Away Home, 16
Of Kings and Things, 23
Old Florist, 43
On Hurricane Jackson, 41
On Sweet Killen Hill, 194

On the Death of Friends in
    Childhood, 236
one winter afternoon, 32
Only for Me, 184

Pancho Villa, 76
Party, The, 139
Peepers in Our Meadow, The,
    208
Picnic, The, 187
Pike, 258
Ploughing on Sunday, 117

Questioning Faces, 176

Rain in the Desert, 128
Reason, 54
Recollection, 173
Remorse for Time, The, 158
Road in Kentucky, A, 196
Robin Hood, 162
Romping, 50
Round, The, 4
Running, 161

Sappa Creek, The, 75
Seed Leaves, 89
Serenade, 7
Simultaneously, 222
Sing a Song of Juniper, 5
Sitting in the Woods: A Con-
    templation, 68
Skier, 20
Sleeping Giant, The, 154
Snapshots of a Daughter-in-law
    (Part I), 39
Snowflake, The, 171
Snowy Night, 109
Song, 3
Song, 10
Sophistication, 115
Spring in These Hills, 88

Squall, 120
Stabilities, 19
Storm, The, 126
Storm on the Island, 121
Summer Music, 91
"Summertime and the living
    . . ." 93
Survivor, 103
"Sweet spring is your, 190

Talisman, A, 65
Teacher, A, 56
That Dark Other Mountain, 242
That Sharp Knife, 87
Thaw in the City, 84
Thought-Fox, The, 228
Tightrope Walker, 21
Time to Talk, A, 49
To My Mother, 43
To Nowhere, 262
To Theon from his son Theon,
    51
Traveling through the Dark, 207
Traveller's Curse After Misdi-
    rection, 59
Tree Is Father to the Man, The,
    165
Twice Shy, 193
Twilight at the Zoo, 268

Uncle Death, 62
Unidentified Flying Object, 214
Utah, 67

Was a Man, 253
Washing Windows, 73
Watering the Horse, 170
Whipping, The, 164
Will You, Won't You?, 205
Willow Poem, 102
Winter, 107
Winter is Another Country, 105

Winter Morning, 108
Winter Scene, A, 110
Woman Mourned by Daughters,
    A, 245

Woman with Girdle, 40

Young, 163
You're, 133

A ball will bounce, but less and less. It's not, 22

After snow a lady is out in our garden, 31

Against the stone breakwater, 126

Ah, but a good wife!, 197

Air heaves at matter, 104

All night the wind swept over the house, 108

All through October, 100

All year the flax-dam festered in the heart, 260

Aloft, lightly on fingertips, 248

And summer mornings the mute child, rebellious, 146

And when that ballad lady went, 196

Anywhere I look, 70

A seated statue of himself he seems, 147

A shadow is floating through the moonlight, 255

A silence hovers over the earth, 88

A smoky rain riddles the ocean plains, 92

As the leaves say, 204

A thousand doors ago, 163

A woman who lived, 221

Beautifully Janet slept, 137

Before I melt, 171

Black girl black girl, 189

Blood thudded in my ears. I scuffed, 159

buy me an ounce and i'll sell you a pound, 11

By all the laws, 165

Cat in the cold, so eager to come in, 205

Denied the shelter of air and the power, 234

Down valley a smoke haze, 94

Drifting night in the Georgia pines, 16

Every day, walking the city streets, 263

"Far enough down is China," somebody said, 157

First, you think they are dead, 72

Flower of the flock, 194

From whence cometh song?, 10

Gull, ballast of its wings, 19

Happened like this: it was hot as hell, 244

He hated them all one by one but wanted to show them, 56

He is found with the homeless dogs, 34

He is leading his grandfather under the sun to market, 35

He lives among a dog, 136

Here am I, a shape under a cedar, 68

Here in the scuffled dust, 138

Here lies resting, out of breath, 237

Here something stubborn comes, 89

Here they are. The soft eyes open, 229

Her face like a rain-beaten stone on the day she rolled off, 42

Her scarf *à la* Bardot, 193
He swings down like the flourish
  of a pen, 20
He Was/a brown old man with a
  green thumb, 44
High on the thrilling strand he
  dances, 21
How strange to think of giving
  up all ambition!, 170

I am driving; it is dusk; Minne-
  sota, 74
"I am Pancho Villa," says the
  truck, 76
I carry my keys like a weapon,
  262
If it comes, 266
If the autumn would, 105
If the Owl Calls Again/at dusk,
  226
I imagine this midnight mo-
  ment's forest, 228
In and out the bushes, up the
  ivy, 79
In Breughel's great picture, The
  Kermess, 15
in Just-, 85
In the cold, cold parlor, 238
In the hazy shape of my mind,
  120
I sat all morning in the college
  sick bay, 240
Is it a dream, or not? During my
  fever, 209
I speak of that great house, 212
I spied John Mouldy in his cel-
  lar, 210
I step around a gate of bushes,
  225
"Is there anybody there?" said
  the Traveller, 213

It is a willow when summer is
  over, 102
It is the picnic with Ruth in the
  spring, 187
It's true Mattie Lee, 214
I took the embankment path,
  256
I Was/the girl of the chain letter, 191
I was six when I first saw kittens
  drown, 235

Lambs that learn to walk in
  snow, 83
Laughter of children brings, 140
Love/if not necessary, is essential, 185

May they stumble, stage by
  stage, 59
Mind in its purest play is like
  some bat, 27
Morning opened, 3
Most near, most dear, most
  loved and most far, 43
My Brother Ben's face, thought
  Eugene, 36
My cat, washing her tail's tip, is
  a whorl, 71
My Daddy has paid the rent, 6
My father could go down a
  mountain faster than I, 242
My grandfather said to me, 156
My son has birds in his head,
  141
My son invites me to witness
  with him, 144

Nature's first green is gold, 169
"next to of course god america i,
  57

Nine white chickens come, 78
Nobody planted roses, he recalls, 93
No closer the glove clings to the sweaty hand, 25
Now, not a tear begun, 245
Now do you suppose that bee, 203
Now his nose's bridge is broken, one eye, 41
Now my legs begin to walk, 84
Now the snow, 107

October nights, wild geese string, 102
Of all the weathers wind is King, 116
Old rusty-belly thing will soon be gone, 75
On a ladder, in an old checkered shirt, 73
On an oak in autumn, 103
Once as I travelled through a quiet evening, 174
one winter afternoon, 32
On the most westerly Blasket, 9
On the summer road that ran by our front porch, 52
On warm days in September the high school band, 53

Passing through huddled and ugly walls, 172
Piecemeal the summer dies, 95
Pike, three inches long, perfect, 258
Poised between going on and back, pulled, 24

Quite unexpectedly as Vasserot, 272

Rain/Million-footed requiem of the rain, 129
Ravished arms/Delighted eyes— and all the rest, 177
Reason/Said, Pull her up a bit will you, Mac, I want to unload there, 54
Right down the shocked street with a siren-blast, 77
Robin Hood/When I was twelve, 162

Sandra and that boy that's going to get her in trouble, 55
Shakespeare would have savored his coarse, irate, 45
She has the immaculate look of the new, 134
Silly. All giggles and ringlets and never, 50
Simultaneously, five thousand miles apart, 222
Since Christmas they have lived with us, 135
Sing a song of juniper, 5
Sir, I encountered Death, 233
Skunk cabbage, bloodroot, 4
Sleep at noon. Window blind, 123
Slow May, 88
Slow moves the acid breath of noon, 101
Snow falling and night falling fast, oh, fast, 111
Softly the crane's foot crumples a star, 173
Sometimes I envy those, 224
Somewhere nowhere in Utah, a boy by the roadside, 67
Summer is all a green air, 91
"sweet spring is your, 190

That hump of a man bunching chrysanthemums, 43

The beauty of manhole covers— what of that?, 66

The child at winter sunset, 176

The first whimper of the storm, 119

The fox he came lolloping, lolloping, 80

The full moon half way up the sky, 206

The great wrought-iron gates have been, 268

The heart, that hideous bear, 181

The house was shaken by a rising wind, 124

The huge red-buttressed mesa over yonder, 128

The jangle of the jeering crows, 265

The lanky hank of a she in the inn over there, 58

The man is clothed, 86

The morning after, 219

The most stupendous show they ever gave, 223

The noses are running at our house, 110

The old man, listening to the careful, 198

The old woman across the way, 164

The rain of a night and a day and a night, 130

The sad seamstress, 37

The steady heart, which in its steadiness, 243

The still scene scintillates, 109

The tin-type tune the locusts make, 7

The trees turn, 99

The way at night these piping peepers, 208

The whiskey on your breath, 14

The white cock's tail, 117

The whole day long, under the walking sun, 154

The wind billowing out the seat of my britches, 145

The winter owl banked just in time to pass, 176

Then it was dark in Illinois, the small boy, 8

"Theon to his father Theon greetings. Another, 51

There was a time when I could fly. I swear it, 160

They served tea in the sandpile, together with, 139

Think of the storm roaming the sky uneasily, 118

This afternoon, darling, when you were here, 246

This is like a place, 109

tonite, *thriller* was, 251

Tonight my children hunch, 264

To our ruined vineyard come, 271

Traveling through the dark I found a deer, 207

Two boys uncoached are tossing a poem together, 26

Under a splintered mast, 65

Unwinding the spool of the morning, 151

Was a man, was a two-, 253

Was I surprised!, 62

We are prepared: we build our houses squat, 121

We heard thunder. Nothing great—on high, 155

We shall not ever meet them
 bearded in heaven, 236
What happened to Joey on our
 block, 23
What I remember, 152
What were we playing? Was it
 prisoner's base?, 161
When a friend calls to me from
 the road, 49
When I kiss Eve, 182
When I saw that clumsy crow,
 227
When I was a boy, I used to go
 to bed, 158
When I was a child, 115
When I was twelve in that far
 land, 184
Where peace goes whispering by,
 69

Where were the greenhouses
 going, 122
Why will they never speak, 33
Winter is long in this climate, 84
Wonderful bears that walked my
 room at night, 153

Yes/And in that month when
 Proserpine comes back, 87
You, once a belle in Shreveport,
 39
you a man, man, man, who know
 the other word, 254
You're/Clownlike, happiest on
 your hands, 133
"Your father's gone," my bald
 headmaster said, 241
Your midriff sags toward your
 knees, 40

ABOUT THE COMPILERS

Helen Hill and Agnes Perkins are members of the English department at Eastern Michigan University, in Ypsilanti, where they teach courses in narrative writing and children's literature. NEW COASTS AND STRANGE HARBORS is their first book, but they have collaborated on many projects, including a jointly written paper on the concept of power as a corrupting force in the works of J. R. R. Tolkien. They report that after they had delivered the Tolkien paper, "we discovered to our amusement that some of our colleagues began to have difficulty remembering which of us was which. There *are* similarities: We both are married to English professors of other institutions, we teach similar courses, we both drive VW's, we both have three sons." But there are differences, too. Mrs. Hill grew up in Taunton, Massachusetts, was graduated from Wheaton College in that state, received her M.A. from Brown University, and did further graduate work at the University of Illinois. In addition to teaching, she has worked as an editor on scholarly and literary journals. She has a daughter, three sons, and four grandchildren, and says that her hobbies are "singing madrigals (regularly), and gardening (sporadically)." Mrs. Perkins was born in Helena, Montana, received her B.A. and M.A. from the University of Montana, and has studied at the Breadloaf School in Vermont. She has written advertising copy for a radio station, and been a reporter for the Helena *Independent-Record*. With her husband and their three sons she lives on an old farm south of Ann Arbor.

ABOUT THE ARTISTS

Clare Romano and John Ross are well-known artists who work individually on their prints and paintings and often collaborate when illustrating a book. They are both graduates of Cooper Union School of Art. Clare Romano is an assistant professor of art at Pratt Institute, and John Ross, professor of art at Manhattanville College.

Their prints are in the collections of many major museums, among them the Museum of Modern Art, the Whitney Museum, and the Metropolitan Museum. Recently they co-authored a definitive work on printmaking.

The illustrations in NEW COASTS AND STRANGE HARBORS are collagraphs, a new intaglio technique that is a printed collage made of cardboard, paper, cloth, and traditionally etched zinc plates. The materials are adhered with acrylic gesso, inked and printed on arches paper in an etching press.